Sparkle and Shine: Your One-Week Path to a Glistening Bathroom

Alexis Riley Brooks

Contents

Preface

"Simplicity is the ultimate sophistication." - Leonardo da Vinci

Welcome to Your New Beginning

At the heart of every home, there's a bathroom: that intimate space where your day begins and ends. Yet, for many, keeping it in sparkling condition is a riddle, wrapped in a mystery, inside an enigma. But what if I told you that within a week, you could transform your bathroom from a place of chaos into a serene sanctuary? This is the promise of our journey together—a no-fuss guide to reclaiming your bathroom's shine, tailored for those navigating the waters of household cleaning for the first time.

Born from the realization that many young adults and first-time cleaners face a daunting task, this book is crafted to empower you. I recognized a profound need for a straightforward, foolproof approach after conversations with people just like you. They shared feelings of overwhelm at the prospect of cleaning, fears of judgment from visitors, and a desire for a home they could be proud of. Each story was a thread in the tapestry that inspired this book.

The Essence of Confidence, One Sparkle at a Time

Imagine, if you will, a friend who has just moved into their first apartment, standing perplexed in the cleaning aisle of a store, overwhelmed by the array of products. This friend represents many of us at the start of our domestic journey—eager yet unsure. It was this image that drove me to distill years of cleaning expertise into a concise, one-week path to a glistening bathroom.

The book you're now holding is a compass in the wilderness of cleaning products and methods. It's designed to guide you through, day by day, with practical tasks, tips, and ticks. From mastering the art of decluttering to choosing the right cleaning agents for different surfaces, every piece of advice is aimed at culminating in not just a cleaner bathroom but a boost in your confidence and well-being.

Acknowledgments That Shine Bright

No book is an island, and this guide is the product of countless conversations, experiments, and feedback. Heartfelt thanks go to the many who shared their homes and stories with me, allowing insights into the common hurdles faced by novices. Their experiences were invaluable in shaping this guide. To my mentors and peers in the cleaning and organizing domains, your wisdom and encouragement were the lighthouses guiding this project to shore. And to you, my reader, for choosing to embark on this transformative journey, thank you. Your trust is the highest compliment.

For Whom This Journey Is Crafted

You might be a young adult fresh out of your parental home, a college graduate stepping into the world of independence, or perhaps someone who's never needed to lift a finger due to serviced living conditions. If the thought of keeping your space clean evokes a sense of dread, or if you're facing the prospect of hosting guests for the first time and want to make a great impression, you're in the right place.

There's no prerequisite knowledge required here— just a willingness to learn and transform your space and, by extension, your life.

Embark on this read with an open heart and a sponge in hand. Your bathroom, that often overlooked space, is about to become a source of pride and joy. As you turn these pages, remember: every great change starts with a single step. Or in our case, a single sweep.

Thank you for inviting me into your journey towards a cleaner, brighter space. Let's begin this voyage together towards a bathroom that not only sparkles but also reflects the sophistication in simplicity you truly deserve.

1

Clean Sweep: Conquering the Chaos in One Week

As the early morning sun crept through the frosted glass window, its light lay in a soft square upon the tile. Megan stirred from her slumber and felt the calmness of the day envelop her. The world was quiet, save for the distant song of a sparrow that had found its solace upon the windowsill. She breathed deeply, the scent of lavender from last night's bath lingering like a whispered memory.

Her eyes fell upon the bathroom, where chaos reigned amongst the serenity of her home. Today, it stood as her adversary. To her guests, the looming party was an occasion for joy, but to Megan, it was a silent beacon of the task at hand - the cleaning of the bathroom. The clutter seemed to mock her, the residue of day-to-day life permeating the once pristine space.

She remembered her mother's house, where surfaces gleamed, and each item held its breath in rightful place. Her hands moved as if with their own memory, tucking toothbrushes back into cups, aligning bottles of creams, and positioning towels with purposeful precision. The counter, now bare, invited the cloth in her hand to dance across its surface, removing every smudge, every trace of neglect.

Megan attacked the grime buildup around the faucet with a stubborn resolve. Water stains held fast, but the gentle abrasion of her chosen tool, a paste made of baking soda and vinegar, began to break their grip. She thought of her grandmother, who seemed to defeat dirt with a mere glance. From her, Megan had learned that a concoction of household ingredients often outdid the mightiest of store-bought cleansers. Now, as the faucet began to regain its lost shine, Megan allowed herself a small smile of victory.

As she scrubbed the tile grout, a rhythm developed, a tempo that matched her heartbeat. Her movements were systematic, the grout lines lengthening like piano keys under the touch of her brush. In this moment, the physical act of cleaning converged with the fluidity of a dance, her body moving from one end of the shower to the other with grace. The white began to reemerge, stark against the grey of aged soap and hard water.

She stepped back, surveying her work. The bathroom, her once unruly foe, had yielded to her will. Yet the morning was slipping away, the sparrow's song a reminder of fleeting time. Megan pondered whether her guests would even notice the gleam of the tile, the strategic placement of the hand soap, or the pure scent of cleanliness that now filled the room. Did her relentless pursuit of perfection serve as a refuge from her thoughts, or did it distract her from the moments that life offered outside these four walls? Would her memories of today be of triumph over a cluttered space, or would they be clouded by the dust she chased away?

As the light in the bathroom grew bolder, reflecting off the surfaces she had polished, what did it reveal about the nature of our daily battles, the ones that stir quietly within us?

Dive Right In: Transforming the Mundane into the Magnificent

Embarking on the journey of transforming your bathroom from cluttered chaos to a sanctuary of sparkle might seem daunting at first, but with the right approach, it's not just attainable—it's downright simple. This segment of our book is your golden ticket to mastering bathroom cleanliness without feeling overwhelmed. **Key to this conquest is a systematic method that not only simplifies the cleaning process but elevates it to an act of rejuvenating your living space.**

First and foremost, let's debunk the myth: a pristine bathroom does not require endless hours or expert-level skills. What it demands is a strategic approach that begins with decluttering and ends with a glistening space. From navigating the mess to zeroing in on what really matters, we'll guide you through every step, ensuring you're equipped with the techniques that make a difference. Here's the exciting part—we achieve this transformative feat in just one week.

Declutter and Prepare: The Foundation of a Brilliant bathroom is more than just removing unnecessary items; it sets the stage for efficiency and effectiveness. Consider the satisfaction of revealing the potential of your space by simply organizing and prioritizing. **This preparation is crucial;** it's akin to an artist setting up their canvas, promising a masterpiece upon completion.

Now, tackling the actual cleaning might seem like stepping into uncharted waters. However, identifying key areas to focus on can drastically cut down the time and effort involved. It's not about cleaning harder, but smarter, targeting spots that accumulate the most grime and utilizing techniques that deliver maximum impact with minimum fuss. This principle is not just about achieving cleanliness in the moment; it's about setting a foundation that makes future cleaning sessions far less intimidating.

Developing an efficient cleaning strategy is akin to mastering a recipe. Just as a chef has a method to their madness, so too will you, turning what might have initially seemed overwhelming into a straightforward, almost effortless routine. **Efficiency is the name of the game;** by optimizing your efforts, you minimize the time invested while maximizing the sparkle and shine.

A Week to Sparkle: A Step by Step Guide

Step 1: Declutter and Remove Excess Items (30 minutes)

Start your mission by liberating your space from anything superfluous. Sorting items into categories and saying goodbye to the unnecessary not only clears physical space but also declutters the mind, setting a positive tone for the journey ahead.

Step 2: Empty and Clean Cabinets and Drawers (1 hour)

Venturing into the depths of cabinets and drawers can unearth forgotten treasures—or just more clutter. Cleaning these spaces not only provides a fresh start but also allows for a moment of organization that will streamline future searches for bathroom essentials.

Step 3: Clear Countertops and Surfaces (30 minutes)

A clear countertop is a visual and functional delight, signaling cleanliness and order. This step is not merely about aesthetics; it significantly reduces the time required for future cleanings by minimizing clutter.

Step 4: Clean and Organize Shower and Tub (1 hour)

Addressing the shower and tub can be the most labor-intensive part, but it's also remarkably rewarding. Sparkling fixtures and tiles not only beautify the bathroom but also contribute to a healthier, mold-free environment.

Step 5: Sweep and Mop the Floor (30 minutes)

Finishing with the floors seals the deal, erasing any traces of the cleaning process itself and leaving nothing but cleanliness behind. This final touch brings the whole effort together, showcasing a bathroom that doesn't just look clean but feels genuinely refreshed.

Each step, meticulously crafted to build upon the previous, ensures a comprehensive approach to bathroom cleanliness. **What makes this process stand out is its adaptability;** whether you're maintaining the sparkle or aiming for a transformative clean, the principles remain the same. By the end of this week, not only will you have a bathroom that gleams, but you'll also possess a methodology that can be applied universally, ensuring lasting cleanliness and a sense of accomplishment.

Remember, the aim is not merely a clean bathroom but a refreshed mindset regarding cleaning itself. View each task not as a chore but as a stepping stone towards a cleaner, more serene living environment. **It's about transforming a mundane task into an opportunity for renewal and relaxation.**

By adopting these practices, you're not just cleaning your bathroom; you're embracing a lifestyle that values order, cleanliness, and the joy of stepping into a room that sparkles. This isn't just about the end result; it's about the journey there—a journey that we promise will be far more rewarding and less daunting than you might have imagined.

Understand How to Declutter and Prepare the Bathroom for an Effective Cleaning Session

Decluttering the bathroom before a cleaning session is much like preparing a canvas before painting. Just as a painter needs a clean, smooth surface to create a masterpiece, cleaning a bathroom efficiently requires starting with a space that is free of unnecessary clutter. This initial step is not just about removing objects but about assessing what actually needs to be there. Visualize the bathroom not as a storage space, but as a sanctuary of cleanliness and relaxation. Every item that doesn't contribute to this vision potentially clutters the space, making the cleaning process more cumbersome and less effective.

To begin, one must tackle the tangible chaos: expired products, half-empty bottles of rarely used lotions, and miscellaneous items that have found their temporary home on countertops. Sorting these out isn't just a matter of space; it's about creating an environment where cleanliness can thrive. Imagine trying to nurture a garden but finding it overrun with weeds. Just as you would clear the weeds to allow the plants to grow, removing clutter allows your bathroom to shine.

In the spirit of efficiency, consider this decluttering phase as laying the groundwork. Once the counters are cleared and cabinets emptied of non-essentials, cleaning becomes a straightforward task, not a daunting challenge. This step ensures that when it's time to scrub and polish, every swipe of the cloth and every spray of cleaner is maximized. It's the difference between navigating through an obstacle course and walking a clear path; the latter is undeniably faster and simpler.

Boldly put: a decluttered bathroom sets the stage for a smooth and effective cleaning session.

A Tidy Triumph: A Step-by-Step Guide to Focusing Your Cleaning Efforts

Step 1: Declutter and Remove Excess Items The battle against bathroom chaos begins with a purge. Clear the battlefield - your countertops, shower caddies, and cabinets - of unneeded items. Like a sculptor removing excess marble to reveal the statue within, eliminate expired products, infrequently used potions, and unwieldy stacks of towels. The goal is not just to simplify your cleaning process but to rediscover and emphasize the space and functionality of your bathroom.

Step 2: Empty and Clean Cabinets and Drawers Imagine each cabinet and drawer as a small chapter in the story of your home. By clearing these spaces, we get the opportunity to rewrite these chapters - this time with clarity and purpose. Wipe down each surface, remove the remnants of past spills, and organize what remains. It's not just cleaning; it's curating your environment to reflect a more organized, serene version of life.

Step 3: Clear Countertops and Surfaces The open landscapes of your countertops hold more than just your daily essentials - they hold the potential for a clean, welcoming space. By clearing and cleaning these areas, you transform them from cluttered stages of morning haste into serene platforms of tranquility and order. It's about setting a stage where cleanliness is the star of the show.

Step 4: Clean and Organize Shower and Tub Dive into the heart of your bathroom - the shower and tub. These are not just places of cleanliness but sanctuaries of relaxation. Scrubbing away the grime and organizing your bathing essentials is akin to polishing the gems of your bathroom. It's where the essence of a sparkling bathroom truly comes to life.

Step 5: Sweep and Mop the Floor Finishing with the floors grounds the entire cleaning process. Just as a painter ensures the edges of their canvas are neat, attending to the corners and expanses of your bathroom floor finalizes the masterpiece of cleanliness. It's the culminating step in transforming your bathroom from a cluttered space to a tranquil retreat.

Could focusing on these key areas be the secret to transforming your bathroom cleaning from a chore to an achievement?

Develop an Efficient Cleaning Strategy That Maximizes Effort and Minimizes Time

The pathway to efficient cleaning is not unlike planning a well-organized route before embarking on a journey. The most direct route, equipped with clear directions and devoid of unnecessary detours, ensures a timely arrival at your destination. Just so, a well-planned cleaning strategy streamlines the process, ensuring each action is purposeful and each effort yields maximum results.

Imagine your cleaning supplies as an arsenal of tools, each selected not for its own sake, but for its utility and effectiveness. By choosing the right tools and cleaning agents for the job, you ensure that no time is wasted on ineffective solutions. This is where knowledge becomes power; understanding the most efficient way to tackle each task ensures that effort is not just expended, but invested wisely.

The true art of efficient cleaning lies in the flow of tasks. Starting high and working your way down ensures that any dirt or debris that falls during cleaning does not soil already clean surfaces. It's like painting a portrait; you wouldn't start with the intricate details without first outlining the broad strokes. Similarly, in cleaning, by structuring your efforts logically, you ensure that each step complements the next, reducing the need for redundant work.

Sweep of Genius: Crafting Your Cleaning Strategy

Step 1: Declutter and Remove Excess Items Everything begins with simplicity. By removing the clutter, you create an environment where cleanliness can flourish unabated. Think of it as priming the canvas before you begin to paint—essential for the final masterpiece to take shape.

Step 2: Empty and Clean Cabinets and Drawers Organizing your storage areas not only aids in finding your necessities but also in maintaining cleanliness. It's akin to organizing a library—every book has its place, and the order facilitates both beauty and utility.

Step 3: Clear Countertops and Surfaces The surfaces we interact with most should be the bastions of cleanliness. By keeping these areas not just clutter-free but sanitized, you're ensuring that your bathroom isn't just clean, but healthy too.

Step 4: Clean and Organize Shower and Tub This sacred space deserves special attention. A clean and organized shower area not only promotes health but also enhances relaxation. It's cleaning with a purpose beyond the surface—aiming for well-being.

Step 5: Sweep and Mop the Floor Concluding with the floors ensures that every part of your bathroom has been touched by your cleaning efforts. It seals the deal on your commitment to not just cleanliness but to creating a haven in your home.

Untangling the efficiency of your cleaning strategy can not only shorten your cleaning time but also heighten the sense of peace in your bathroom space.

In synthesizing our exploration of decluttering preparation, focused cleaning efforts, and an efficient cleaning strategy, it becomes evident that the mastery of these three arenas acts as the cornerstone to transforming a daunting task into a series of purposeful actions.

Embrace the Transformation of Your Bathroom

Now that you have delved into the world of bathroom cleaning, it's time to unleash the potential of your space. By mastering the art of decluttering, honing in on key cleaning areas, and developing a strategic cleaning process, you are well on your way to conquering the chaos in your bathroom.

Ready to Sparkle and Shine?

In the upcoming chapters, you will uncover a treasure trove of cleaning secrets and techniques that will not only revolutionize your bathroom but also transform your approach to cleaning. Get ready to unlock a realm of efficiency and effectiveness that will leave you feeling empowered and proud of your sparkling sanctuary.

Stay tuned for expert tips and foolproof methods that will make maintaining a glistening bathroom a breeze. Imagine stepping into a bathroom that radiates cleanliness and serenity every day, with minimal effort on your part.

Say goodbye to the days of feeling overwhelmed by the prospect of cleaning your bathroom. With the tools and knowledge provided in this book, you'll soon realize that achieving a pristine bathroom is well within your reach. Get ready to embark on a journey of transformation and make your bathroom a place of comfort, beauty, and cleanliness.

Get ready to sparkle and shine like never before!

2

The Essential Arsenal: Must-Have Tools for a Sparkling Throne

The morning sun breached the blinds, casting stripes of light across the bathroom's tiled floor. Flora stood there, a fortress of cleaning supplies amassed on the countertop. Her reflection in the mirror showed furrowed brows as she eyed the grime in the grout, the water spots on the faucet, the soap scum on the shower door. She sighed, the burden of tackling the mess heavy on her shoulders.

In her hands, a spray bottle labeled with a promise to erase all traces of dirt and mildew — a costly concoction she had begun to doubt. Her mind wandered to the cupboard beneath the sink, a maze of products each boasting specificity: one for tiles, another for glass, a creamy solution for chrome fixtures. She remembered her mother's cupboard, a minimalist's palette — white vinegar, baking soda, and a stout scrub brush had been her totems of cleanliness.

A knock on the door sliced through her contemplation, and her little one's voice, playful yet insistent, reminded her that her cleaning ritual was encroaching on their day. Flora placed the spray bottle down, the click of it settling felt like the closing of a chapter. She would pare down, she resolved; she would return to simplicity for the sake of time, money, and space. A revelation unfolded in her mind, one that whispered of the unnecessary.

She removed the unused products one by one, mentally acknowledging the unnecessary excess, the lure of aggressive marketing that had seduced her into thinking more was better. Her bathroom appeared larger now, the space beneath the sink too. A sense of calm settled as she selected a few essentials to remain: a bottle of all-purpose cleaner, a jug of vinegar, a tin of baking soda, and a bundle of rags — this Spartan array seemed to promise a newfound efficiency.

Kneeling by the bathtub, Flora scrubbed with newfound purpose. The scent of vinegar filled the air, sharp but reassuring. Her movements became rhythmic, the scouring transforming from chore to meditation. The simpler toolkit liberated her, her thoughts shifting to the new possibilities that this reclaimed time might birth. The cleaning finished, tiles gleamed, the glass shone clear, and the chrome sparkled. Less had indeed been more.

As she rinsed out the cloth and placed it to dry, a question extended its roots in her mind. Had the world complicated the straightforward under the guise of progress, and what other facets of her life could be made richer by choosing less?

Unlock the Secret to a Sparkling Bathroom

Let's dive straight into the heart of creating a gleaming bathroom sanctuary without cluttering your cabinets with expensive, one-trick cleaning products. Surprisingly, the path to a spotless bathroom doesn't wind through aisles laden with specialty cleaners. Instead, it hinges on a simple, yet transformative, set of tools that won't break the bank. **Understanding the power of multipurpose items** is the cornerstone of our journey. Armed with just these, tackling any bathroom mess becomes an effortless task.

The beauty of this approach lies in its simplicity and effectiveness. Imagine having a cleaning kit so streamlined, yet so versatile, that it could address everything from lime scale to soap scum with equal ease. First, **recognizing which products are superfluous** is a critical step in refining your cleaning arsenal. This not only frees space but also redirects focus to what truly matters – effective, stress-free cleaning routines.

Among the essentials, a few standout products promise to transform your bathroom from grimy to gleaming without the accompanying sticker shock. These include a quality microfiber cloth, a durable scrub brush, and a reliable all-purpose cleaner. Selecting these with care ensures that you're equipped to tackle a wide range of cleaning tasks, making the seemingly arduous mission of maintaining a sparkling bathroom surprisingly manageable.

Proper storage and maintenance of these tools are equally important. Just as a craftsman cares for their tools to ensure longevity, so too should the prudent cleaner. Simple practices like rinsing brushes after use and allowing them to dry properly can significantly extend their useful life, ensuring they're ready and effective for each cleaning session.

As we strip away the complexity often associated with cleaning, we uncover the foundations of confidence in our cleaning abilities. It's not about having the most cleaners or gadgets; it's about wielding the right ones with purpose and knowledge. This approach not only simplifies the act of cleaning but elevates it, transforming it into a task that feels less like a chore and more like an empowering act of care for your space.

Remember, the aim here is not just to clean but to do so with efficiency and poise. By becoming selective about our tools, we learn to cut through the noise and focus on what truly contributes to a clean, inviting bathroom. This not only saves time but also fosters a sense of accomplishment and wellbeing. After all, a sparkling bathroom is a source of pride, a haven of cleanliness that speaks volumes about our dedication to our homes and ourselves.

Let this chapter serve as a blueprint to reclaim your time and energy. By focusing on quality, multi-use tools, and learning to streamline your approach, you set the stage for a bathroom that not only shines but also reflects a smarter, more thoughtful way of cleaning. Embrace this path, and watch as your bathroom transforms into a testament to the power of simplicity and efficiency.

In the pursuit of a sparkling bathroom, one might believe that a treasure chest of expensive cleaners and gadgets is essential. However, this chapter unfolds the truth about the minimal, versatile warriors that can effortlessly conquer the realm of bathroom grime. The key to an immaculately clean bathroom lies in understanding that less is often more. With just a few affordable and multipurpose cleaning products, you can tackle most bathroom messes with surprising ease.

Imagine each mess as a challenging puzzle. Just as a few well-chosen puzzle pieces can beautifully complete the picture, a carefully selected arsenal of cleaning supplies can address numerous cleaning tasks. Instead of a closet full of seldom-used specialized cleaners, a compact yet versatile kit can become your go-to weapon against dirt and grime. This not only simplifies your cleaning routine but also saves valuable storage space and money.

Among the champions of this arsenal, white vinegar stands out for its remarkable versatility and affordability. A natural disinfectant, it can effortlessly cleanse and deodorize surfaces, tackle mold, and even dissolve hard water stains. Baking soda is another hero, known for its gentle scrubbing power and its ability to neutralize odors. When these two are combined, they create a formidable duo that can tackle a wide range of cleaning tasks, from brightening grout to removing soap scum.

Another key player is a quality microfiber cloth, which can trap and remove dust and dirt with minimal effort and without the need for additional chemicals. Add a good old-fashioned scrub brush into the mix, and you have a complete set that can handle nearly every challenge your bathroom can throw at you. This approach not only champions environmental consciousness by reducing chemical use but also champions your wallet.

In essence, the foundation of an effective cleaning strategy doesn't lie in a plethora of specialized products but in a few, well-chosen allies. By understanding the strengths and applications of each product, you can keep your bathroom sparkling with minimal effort and expense. **The cornerstone of a sparkling throne is not the quantity but the quality and versatility of your cleaning arsenal.**

As we delve deeper into our cleaning toolkit, it's crucial to recognize not just what to include but what to leave out. The market is flooded with specialized cleaning products, each promising miracle solutions for specific cleaning woes. Yet, in reality, these products often clutter our spaces and empty our wallets while not significantly improving our cleaning outcomes.

One may wonder, then, how to differentiate between the essentials and the superfluous. Consider the appliances in a kitchen; while a toaster, a stove, and a refrigerator are indispensable, how often do you truly need that yogurt maker or avocado slicer? Similarly, in our cleaning kit, some items serve as the bread and butter, while others are merely garnishing, rarely used and easily replaced with a little creativity and elbow grease.

Streamlining your cleaning kit requires a mindful evaluation of each product's utility. Take, for example, the myriad of surface cleaners available. Many boast unique formulas for every type of surface in your bathroom, from tiles to glass to wood. Yet, a versatile all-purpose cleaner can often do the job just as effectively, without the need to juggle multiple bottles and sprays.

The art of streamlining lies in identifying multitaskers that offer broad-spectrum efficacy. By doing so, you simplify your cleaning process, making it quicker and more efficient. This shift towards simplification not only makes the cleaning task less daunting but also more sustainable, as it reduces waste and minimizes the environmental impact of our cleaning practices.

A journey towards minimalism in our cleaning supplies is not about compromise but about making intelligent choices that enhance efficiency and effectiveness. It's about refusing to be swayed by marketing tactics that push for more when, in fact, less can often achieve the same, if not better, results.

Could recognizing and eliminating the unnecessary from our lives, beyond just our cleaning kits, be the epiphany we need to lead simpler, more fulfilling lives?

Maintaining a lean, efficient cleaning arsenal is not just about what we choose to include; it's also about caring for and storing these essentials properly. Like any tool, cleaning supplies have their lifespan and effectiveness, which can be significantly affected by how they are stored.

Picture a garden where each plant needs proper soil, sunlight, and water to thrive. Similarly, each cleaning product and tool has its optimal storage condition that ensures its efficacy and longevity. For instance, microfiber cloths need to be washed without fabric softener to maintain their dust-trapping abilities, while brushes and sponges should be stored in a dry place to prevent mold growth.

Proper storage extends beyond preserving the life of our tools; it's also about safety. Many cleaning agents, even the more natural ones like vinegar, need to be kept out of reach of children and pets. Furthermore, ensuring that lids and caps are securely fastened can prevent spills and leaks, which might damage storage areas or pose risks to household members.

The philosophy of "a place for everything and everything in its place" holds true here. By dedicating specific, easily accessible spots for cleaning supplies, you not only keep them in optimal condition but also make the cleaning process smoother and faster. This strategic organization eliminates time wasted searching for tools and products, allowing for more efficient cleaning sessions.

Integrating these three key objectives—identifying essential multipurpose products, eliminating the unnecessary, and proper maintenance and storage—creates a streamlined, effective cleaning routine that simplifies your life and elevates your bathroom to a consistently sparkling state.

Summary and Next Steps

In the journey to a gleaming bathroom, we've uncovered the **essential arsenal** needed to conquer dirt and grime efficiently. By **focusing on a select few versatile products**, you can achieve remarkable results without breaking the bank. Remember, it's not about the number of items in your cleaning kit, but rather the **effectiveness of each product** you choose to use.

Quality Over Quantity

As we've seen, it's not about having a surplus of fancy products but rather selecting **quality, multipurpose items** that can tackle various cleaning tasks. By investing in **affordable, versatile supplies**, you streamline your cleaning routine, making it both **efficient and cost-effective**.

Streamlining for Success

Now that you know which products are truly indispensable, you can eliminate unnecessary items that clutter your space and complicate your cleaning process. Keep your arsenal **simple and functional**, focusing on the tried-and-true essentials that deliver **consistent results**.

Maintenance Matters

Lastly, proper storage and maintenance of your cleaning supplies are crucial to ensure their longevity and effectiveness. By storing products in a **cool, dry place** away from direct sunlight and moisture, you preserve their potency. **Regularly checking expiration dates** and replacing old or expired products is key to maintaining a **high standard of cleanliness** in your bathroom.

As you commence your one-week journey to a spotless sanctuary, armed with the knowledge of essential cleaning tools and techniques, remember that a sparkling bathroom is within your reach with just a few strategic choices. It's time to roll up your sleeves, grab your trusty supplies, and let's get that bathroom shining!

3

The Weekly Warriors: Balancing Deep Cleans and Daily Touch-Ups

It was a bright mid-morning in a quiet suburb where the wind played a gentle tune as it passed through the leaves. Emily stood in the midst of her bathroom, arms akimbo, brow furrowed, surrounded by a horde of cleaning supplies. The sponge in her hand was dripping with the weight of decision, as she contemplated the strategy to transform this space from its worn state to a gleaming sanctuary.

She had a memory, fresh as the morning dew, of a time when the bathroom shone, when the tiles reflected her smiling face and the chrome fixtures sparkled with pride. But those days seemed as distant as the calm blue of the ocean that lay beyond her bathroom window. There, beyond the pane, seagulls called and swooped as if urging her to find the balance she sought – one between the tide of regular upkeep and the wave of deep cleaning.

As she began to wipe down the countertop, her grandmother's words floated back to her. "Keep on top of the mess, dearie," she had said with a knowing smile, "A stitch in time saves nine." The tiles received her methodical scrubbing, while her mind worked to stitch her plan together. Her grandmother's house had always been impeccable; the result was not just of rigorous deep cleanings, but of tablespoons of daily care mixed into life's simmering pot.

A glance towards the shower curtain, splattered with water stains, reminded her of her friends who rallied by the banner of deep cleaning, devoting entire days to what she considered a Herculean task. Their bathrooms, too, emerged from these sessions as pristine as a hospital ward, but Emily questioned the sustainability of that battle against bacteria and grime. Would her energy not be better invested in a little and often approach?

Her hand paused, the sponge hesitated mid-air, as she heard a child's laughter from the bedroom. Her son, blissfully unaware of the microbial universe lurking on doorknobs and light switches, served as her daily reminder that while a clean home is a healthy home, a home is meant to be lived in.

The warm light shifted across the tiled floor as if pointing toward a decision. Perhaps the secret lay in a routine that embraced both philosophies – a rhythm of life that danced between swift, daily wipe-downs and the crescendo of occasional deep cleans. Could it be that this middle path was the way to keep both her sanity and her sanctuary?

Emily rinsed the sponge and watched the suds spiral away down the drain, lost to the same question that winds its way through the minds of all who take pride in their homes. How does one master the art of maintaining the daily sparkle without losing themselves to the scour of the deep clean?

Embrace the Balance: The Art of Consistent Bathroom Brilliance

Navigating the world of bathroom cleanliness can often feel like charting a course through uncharted waters. For many, the quest for a perpetually pristine bathroom is fraught with confusion—*do I clean a little every day or dedicate hours for a deep clean?* Here lies the heart of our discussion: the equilibrium between daily maintenance and the indispensable deep clean. This balance is not just about keeping appearances; it's a strategic approach to a healthy, sparkling bathroom that serves as a haven rather than a headache.

Understanding the significance of a balanced cleaning schedule is the first step on this journey. Regular upkeep, as mundane as it may seem, plays a crucial role in preventing the accumulation of dirt and grime. It's the shield that protects your bathroom from becoming a breeding ground for unwanted guests like mold and bacteria. But, while daily touch-ups are your first line of defense, they skim only the surface of what truly lies beneath. Here, the profound importance of a periodic deep clean comes to light, targeting those concealed corners and unseen expanses where germs find sanctuary.

Creating a balanced cleaning regimen might sound like a task reserved for the overly meticulous. However, this couldn't be further from the truth. It's about setting a rhythm that keeps your bathroom in a constant state of readiness—ready to dazzle, ready to comfort. Imagine waking up each morning to a bathroom that not only looks clean but feels deeply, refreshingly pure. This doesn't require endless hours; rather, it's about smart, focused efforts that culminate in a consistently welcoming space.

To dive into the specifics, let's break down key areas based on their cleaning needs. **High-traffic zones**—the sink, the toilet seat, and the floor—demand daily attention. These are the areas that interact most frequently with users, and as such, they're prime real estate for bacteria and stains. A quick wipe-down, a swift sweep, and perhaps a brisk mop can work wonders in maintaining their cleanliness.

On the flip side, there are niches within your bathroom that call for the occasional deep dive. Think about the grout between your tiles, the inside of your sink cabinet, or even the water fixtures. These sections might not require daily scrutiny, but without regular deep cleaning, they can significantly detract from your bathroom's overall hygiene and aesthetic.

Integrating both strategies into your cleaning repertoire is easier than it sounds. Start by designating specific days for more extensive tasks, making them non-negotiable appointments with your bathroom. This structured approach not only spreads out the workload but also instills a habit—if Monday is mirror day, then let there be no exception. For daily tasks, create a pre-bedtime or post-morning routine that ensures these areas never miss out on their deserved attention.

Embarking on this balanced path to bathroom brilliance is more than a chore; it's a commitment to a lifestyle where cleanliness and health play a pivotal role. It empowers you not just to react to dirt and clutter but to preemptively maintain a space that's always inviting. And so, as you arm yourself with these insights, remember that in the realm of bathroom upkeep, it's the steady rhythm of daily touches combined with the thorough cadence of deep cleaning that creates a symphony of cleanliness. Let this harmony guide you to a bathroom that not just sparkles and shines but breathes wellness into your home.

Crafting a Balanced Cleaning Schedule

Creating a balanced cleaning schedule that combines both daily touch-ups and deep cleans is akin to tending a garden. Just as a garden needs regular watering and weeding to thrive, along with occasional deep soil nourishment, your bathroom requires a similar approach to maintain its sparkle. This isn't just about aesthetics; it's about cultivating a hygienic, welcoming space that reflects care and attention.

Regular maintenance of the bathroom can seem like a daunting daily chore, but it's really about setting quick, manageable tasks. Wiping down surfaces, ensuring towels are hung to dry, and clearing clutter can prevent the kind of buildup that demands heavy-duty cleaning. These are the light, frequent brushstrokes that keep the canvas of your bathroom bright and inviting.

Then, there's the deep clean – a thorough, methodical scrubbing that reaches the nooks and crannies, disinfects, and restores. This deeper level of cleaning targets the unseen, the overlooked, where mold, mildew, and bacteria like to hide. It's the comprehensive overhaul that ensures your bathroom isn't just clean on the surface, but deep down where it counts. Planning a deep clean weekly or bi-weekly, depending on your household's use and needs, is crucial for maintaining the health and hygiene of your space.

Think of your cleaning schedule as a balance beam. On one end, daily quick wipes and tidies. On the other, the hefty, deep-cleaning sessions. Both are essential, and keeping them in harmony ensures your bathroom remains a sanctuary, not a source of stress. The trick is finding your rhythm and sticking to it, adjusting as necessary to suit your lifestyle and household.

The key to a consistently clean and welcoming bathroom lies in balancing regular upkeep with thorough, periodic deep cleans.

The Significance of Regular Upkeep

Imagine your bathroom as a canvas, each day adding strokes of toothpaste splatters, fingerprint smudges, and water spots. Without regular attention, the canvas becomes cluttered and chaotic. Regular upkeep acts as the eraser, gently wiping away the daily marks, preventing the artwork from becoming overwhelmed. This daily ritual of maintenance prevents dirt and grime from setting in, making your deep cleaning sessions less about restoring order from chaos and more about enhancing the bathroom's innate sparkle.

Regular upkeep is more than just a hygiene practice; it's a proactive measure against wear and tear. Water, if left on fixtures and tiles, can cause long-term damage, leading to the need for expensive repairs or replacements. By wiping down surfaces daily, you're not just cleaning; you're preserving the life and luster of your bathroom's fixtures and finishes.

In the realm of bathroom cleaning, prevention is indeed better than cure. Allowing soap scum, hard water deposits, and mildew to build up not only creates more work for you but also provides breeding grounds for germs and bacteria. Daily touch-ups ensure that these unwelcome guests don't become permanent residents in your space.

Yet, regular maintenance isn't only about cleanliness and prevention; it's also a psychological boon. A clean and organized bathroom sets a tone of tranquility and order for your day. It can transform a space from being a mere functional area into a personalized retreat where you rejuvenate and prepare for the challenges ahead.

Consistency in your cleaning routine fosters a sense of pride and accomplishment. It's the foundation upon which the health and hygiene of your bathroom rest. Ensuring that everyday messes are promptly dealt with means that when it's time for a deep clean, the process is less about tackling overwhelming grime and more about refining and refreshing.

Could recognizing the value of this daily discipline be the turning point in how we perceive and manage our home environments?

Prioritizing Cleaning Efforts

Identifying which areas of your bathroom require daily attention versus those that need a deeper, less frequent touch can be likened to knowing when to water your plants and when they need pruning. Certain spots, like your sink and countertops, are high-traffic zones. They collect remnants of our daily routines — toothpaste splatters, soap residues, water spots — and thus, demand daily wiping. It's the equivalent of watering your indoor plants; a little daily care goes a long way.

On the other end, there are areas that call for the metaphorical pruning — the deep cleaning. Think about the grout between tiles, the showerhead, or the hidden corners behind the toilet. These are the spots that, while not requiring daily attention, become sanctuaries for grime and bacteria over time if neglected. Scheduling a periodic deep clean targets these areas, ensuring that your bathroom is not just clean on the surface but in every nook and cranny.

Creating a targeted cleaning schedule starts with understanding the dynamics of your bathroom. Just as certain plants need more sunlight, certain areas of your bathroom demand more focus. Surfaces like faucets and door handles, for example, are touched frequently and therefore, are hotspots for germs. They benefit from daily disinfecting to curb the spread of illness.

The goal is to strike a balance; not every corner of your bathroom needs your attention every day. By apportioning your efforts wisely, cleaning becomes less of a chore and more of a simple routine. This approach ensures that your bathroom remains a sanctuary of cleanliness and comfort, without the process feeling overwhelming or time-consuming.

Balancing between daily upkeep and periodic deep cleans, while prioritizing key areas based on their use and exposure, is essential for maintaining a hygienic, welcoming bathroom environment.

Finding Your Balance

Balancing the daily touch-ups with deep cleans isn't just about keeping your bathroom looking immaculate; it's about creating a space that's truly clean and healthy for you and your family. **Consistency is key** in maintaining this balance.

Stay Ahead of the Grime

Regular upkeep is your best defense against dirt and grime taking over your bathroom. By tackling small messes promptly, you prevent them from becoming larger problems that require intensive cleaning.

Targeted Attention

Certain areas in your bathroom, like the sink and toilet, require more frequent cleaning to keep them free of germs and looking their best. **Focusing on these high-traffic spots during daily touch-ups can make a significant difference in overall cleanliness.**

Deep Dive

Don't skip out on deep cleaning sessions. These are essential for reaching the nooks and crannies where grime hides and bacteria thrive. **Committing to periodic deep cleans ensures a thorough sanitization of your bathroom,** promoting a healthier environment for you and your loved ones.

Finding Harmony

As you navigate the weekly cleaning routine, remember to find a balance that works for you. **Whether you lean towards daily maintenance or allocate more time for deep cleaning, the key is consistency.** By sticking to a schedule that covers all your cleaning needs, you'll enjoy a sparkling clean bathroom that shines with freshness and hygiene.

4

The Joy of Suds: Cultivating A Cleansing Zen

Maggie shuffled around the cramped kitchen, navigating through piles of unwashed dishes and stacks of bills that loitered like unwanted guests. The soapy water, speckled with food scraps, hinted at a lemon zest, masking the staleness of the room. Tiny suds escaped, floating upwards, weightless and indifferent to the gravity that seemed to tug heavier on her shoulders with each passing day.

She thought about her grandmother's house, the scent of pine cleaner interwoven with the aroma of fresh-baked bread, how the windows gleamed with promise. How had such a sanctuary of cleanliness and order felt like the height of self-care? There was joy in the gleam of the countertops, a strange serenity in the whisper of the broom across the floor. Maggie's breaths unfurled in the warm sudsy haze, contemplating how her own home had become less of a refuge and more of a physical reminder of the chaos that hummed through her life.

Envisioning her bathroom at home, which had become a source of dread, Maggie inhaled deeply as if bracing to dive underwater. She could transform it, surely, from a mere cubicle where mildew had taken a bold residency, into a spa-like haven. But the very task seemed monumental, and yet there was her grandmother's voice, reverberating in her mind, "Take pride in your abode, dear. It's the nest for your soul."

Maggie seized the scrub brush with a newfound conviction, dipping it into the mix of baking soda and vinegar she had concocted after reading about non-toxic cleaners. With every determined stroke against the bathtub's grime, it wasn't just scrubbing; it was an act of reclaiming space, of nurturing her environment, and in a small, meaningful way, caring for herself.

An old radio, perched precariously on the fridge, crooned a melody that seemed oddly fitting for her battle against the bathroom's moldy corners. Her feet tapped to the rhythm, shifting her movement to a dance, and her heart found itself lightening with the tune. She hummed along, feeling oddly triumphant with each tile that sparkled back at her as if in gratitude. A smile broke across her face when she imagined her grandmother nodding in silent approval.

Is it not in the simple act of brushing away the old, making room for the new, that we find our greatest renewal?

Transform Your Space, Transform Your Mind

When embarking on the journey to a spotless bathroom, it's crucial to reimagine the cleaning process as not just another chore, but as a soothing ritual for self-care. Imagine transforming your space into a sanctuary that not only welcomes you but also projects a sense of peace and cleanliness to anyone who enters. This transformation begins with **shifting your perspective** from viewing cleaning as a burdensome task to seeing it as an engaging activity that offers psychological benefits and a tangible reward: a glistening, welcoming space.

Understanding that **cleaning can be a form of self-care** is foundational. It's about caring for your living space and, by extension, yourself. This means embracing the process with enthusiasm and finding joy in the gradual transformation of your bathroom from cluttered and grimy to sparkling and serene. Every scrub, swipe, and polish can be seen as an act of kindness to yourself and those you share your space with. It's about creating an inviting atmosphere that makes you feel proud and tranquil.

Making cleaning enjoyable comes next. This can involve creating personal reward systems for yourself, like indulging in a relaxing bath in your newly cleaned bathroom or treating yourself to a small luxury after completing your cleaning session. Incorporating elements that elevate the experience, such as playing your favorite music or podcasts, can also transform cleaning from a solitary task to a more enjoyable, rhythm-filled dance around the bathroom.

The **psychological benefits** of maintaining a clean and organized space cannot be understated. Studies have shown that clean spaces can significantly impact our mental health, reducing stress and improving focus and creativity. The act of cleaning itself can be meditative, offering a break from the digital overload and constant distractions of our lives. It's about reclaiming control over our physical environment and, by extension, our mental one.

When you start to see cleaning as less of a chore and more as an opportunity for self-improvement and care, you unlock a different experience. Each cleaning session is no longer just about battling dirt and grime; it's about cultivating a space that reflects the best parts of yourself. **This mindset shift** is key to not just enduring the cleaning process, but actively enjoying it.

Thus, the joy found in the suds and the act of cleaning is deeply intertwined with the joy of cultivating a welcoming, clean space. It's a cyclical relationship where one feeds into the other, creating an ever-improving environment that benefits both the physical space and the individual's mental state. This chapter aims to guide you through embracing these insights, turning what might have been perceived as a mundane task into a fulfilling routine that contributes significantly to your overall well-being.

In essence, the approach to cleaning your bathroom, and indeed any area of your life, can be transformed through a **positive mindset, enjoyable practices, and an understanding of its broader benefits.** This isn't just about achieving a glistening bathroom but about fostering a state of mind that sees beauty in the act of caring for and improving one's living space. With each cleaning session, you're not just removing dirt; you're creating a sanctuary that nourishes and rejuvenates.

Transforming Perspective: From Chore to Self-Care

Imagine for a moment the feeling of stepping into a spa, where every detail is curated to promote relaxation and rejuvenation. Now, consider the possibility of evoking a similar sentiment in your own bathroom through the simple act of cleaning. Often, the task of scrubbing and tidying up is viewed as a burden, a mere chore that eats into our precious free time. Yet, with a shift in perspective, this very act can become a form of self-care, an expression of love towards oneself and the home that shelters us.

The transformation begins with understanding. Recognize that a clean environment does far more than offer visual appeal—it nurtures our well-being by creating a sanctuary from the world's chaos. Every stroke of the brush, each sweep of the mop, can be an affirmation of worth and care for one's personal space, turning mundane tasks into a meditative practice.

Consider the humble act of cleansing as gardening. Just as we water plants and remove weeds, ensuring our living space is clean helps us cultivate a healthy environment where well-being can flourish. This analogy underscores the nurturing aspect of cleaning. It's about more than just tidiness; it's about cultivating an environment where our spirits can soar.

Incorporating this mindset shift requires a conscious effort. Start by setting intentions before each cleaning session. Approach the task with gratitude, appreciating the opportunity to enhance your living space. Affirm to yourself that this is not just a chore but a valuable act of self-care that contributes to your overall happiness and peace.

By viewing cleaning as a form of self-care, we transform an ordinary task into an extraordinary act of love for ourselves and our sanctuary.

Cultivating Joy in the Cleaning Process

The prospect of cleaning, particularly a space as intimate and vital as the bathroom, doesn't have to induce a groan. Think of it instead as an artist approaching a canvas, with the opportunity to create a masterpiece of cleanliness and order. How, then, can we infuse this seemingly tedious process with joy? The answer lies in personalizing the experience to transform it into a pleasurable activity.

One effective strategy is the introduction of a personal reward system. Just as children are often motivated by rewards for accomplishing tasks, so too can adults benefit from this incentive. Promise yourself a small reward post-cleaning, whether it's a relaxing bath, a special treat, or time spent with a favorite book. This forms a positive association with the task, making it something to look forward to rather than dread.

Music plays a powerful role in altering our mood and can make the cleaning experience significantly more enjoyable. Creating a cleaning playlist with upbeat, energetic songs can turn the task into a lively dance party. Not only does this make the time pass more quickly, but it also injects a dose of fun into the process, making it something you might actually look forward to.

Personalization extends to the tools and cleaners used as well. Investing in supplies that appeal to you, whether through their fragrance, efficiency, or design, can make a big difference in how you perceive the cleaning task. Using items that you like naturally elevates the experience, making it more satisfying and less of a chore.

Visualization is another powerful method to enhance the cleaning experience. Before beginning, take a moment to visualize the space as you want it to be, focusing on the positive feelings associated with achieving this goal. This mental practice can serve as motivation, driving you to create the welcoming, clean space you envision.

With these strategies in mind, the cleaning process can be transformed from a dreaded chore to an enjoyable, even fulfilling, part of your routine. The key is to find what works best for you, making the task not just bearable, but potentially delightful.

Could tweaking your approach to cleaning be the secret to not only a sparkling bathroom but also to newfound happiness in the process?

The Psychological Boost of Cleanliness

The impact of a clean and organized space on our mental and emotional well-being cannot be overstated. Scientific research has consistently shown that people tend to feel more relaxed, focused, and happy in environments that are orderly. The act of cleaning, then, is not merely about maintaining aesthetics but about nurturing our mental health.

Just as a painter feels a sense of accomplishment upon completing a masterpiece, we too can experience a profound sense of satisfaction from tidying our surroundings. This accomplishment doesn't just result in a visually pleasing environment but also promotes a feeling of control and competence. In essence, the state of our surroundings can mirror and influence our internal state, with cleanliness fostering a sense of peace and renewal.

Consider if the mind was a garden. A cluttered, disorganized space is like a garden overrun with weeds, where beauty is obscured and growth is stifled. Cleaning, in this sense, is the act of weeding our external environment, which in turn, cultivates a healthier, more vibrant mental garden. This analogy highlights the interconnectedness of our physical spaces and psychological states - each can nurture or negate the other.

To leverage the psychological benefits of a clean space, it's crucial to integrate regular cleaning into our routine. Viewing this practice not just as a task but as a valuable component of self-care reinforces its importance and the positive impact it has on our well-being.

Highlighting the importance of a clean and organized space for our mental health underscores the transformative potential of regular cleaning: it's not just about the space itself, but about cultivating a mindset that values and nurtures our overall well-being.

Embrace the Sparkle Within

As we reach the end of this chapter, it's essential to **embrace the transformative power** that a positive mindset can have on your approach to cleaning. By shifting your perspective from viewing cleaning as a mundane task to seeing it as an act of self-care and a way to create a welcoming environment, you open the door to a world of possibilities.

Elevate Your Cleaning Experience

By infusing joy and purpose into your cleaning routine, you not only create a sparkling space but also nurture a sense of accomplishment and well-being within yourself. Remember, each swipe of the cloth, each spritz of cleaner, is an opportunity to show care and respect for your surroundings and yourself.

Cultivate a Cleansing Zen

As you continue on your journey of bathroom beautification, keep in mind that **maintaining a clean and organized**

space is not just about appearances; it's about cultivating a sense of calm and clarity within your home. So next time you embark on your cleaning adventure, put on your favorite tunes, light a candle, and let the joy of suds wash over you. Before you know it, your bathroom will not only sparkle and shine but also radiate the positive energy you've poured into it.

5

Divide and Conquer: Simplifying Your Scrub Routine

The early light of the city morning filtered through the mist, coating everything with a soft glow. Marianne paused, the warmth of her small apartment at her back. The chill of the outside world met her as she stepped over the threshold, juggling keys, a purse, and a resolve to face the day with equanimity. She descended the steps, crisp autumn leaves brushing against her shoes and whispering of transitions.

Inside Marianne's mind, a different sort of cleaning awaited her attention, not dissimilar to the one her apartment required. Thoughts scattered like the toys in her nephew's room after a fervent play session; each one needed picking up, examining, and returning to its rightful place. Today, she decided, she would begin to organize her world, both internally and externally.

The workday passed in a blur of customer greetings and the beep of the cash register. Back at home, in the sanctuary of her kitchen, she faced the enemy of her peace: clutter. As she gathered the dirty dishes and wiped down counters, her mind mirrored her actions, organizing worries into manageable fragments. A plan formed, shimmering with potential. "One thing at a time," she whispered, as if it were a mantra.

By evening, Marianne sat down with paper and pen, not to draft a letter but a map of her upcoming week. Each day held a promise, a task both simple and profound in its singular nature. Mondays were for dusting away doubts and furniture in equal measure, while Tuesdays would see her tackling the floors as well as her tendency to procrastinate. Every stroke of the pen was an act of commitment to a cleaner space and a clearer mind.

Night had fallen fully by the time Marianne placed the finishing touch on her weekly cleaning chart, mundane yet somehow sacred in its intentions. The shadows in her living room were tinged with the satisfaction of knowing what tomorrow would bring. The room hummed quietly with the stillness of readiness, a canvas wiped clean, ready to be painted afresh.

As Marianne settled into the plush cushions of her couch, she wondered how many others lay awake at this hour, contemplating the countless ways to break free from the cobwebs that bound them to inaction. Would they too find solace in routine and the simple pleasure of a well-kept home? And what might such order unlock within their lives, if given the chance?

Transform Bathroom Blues into Sparkles of Success

Imagine walking into your bathroom to find it perpetually gleaming, the kind of clean that sparkles and invites a deep, satisfying breath. For many, the bathroom's constant battle against grime and clutter can feel overwhelming, but it doesn't have to be. The secret to transforming your bathroom from a daunting task into a manageable triumph lies in simplifying your scrub routine through the art of divide and conquer. By breaking down the cleaning process into daily manageable steps, creating an actionable and personalized weekly cleaning plan, and learning tips to avoid procrastination and maintain consistency, you'll find that a clean bathroom is not just possible; it's easily attainable.

Mastering the art of breaking down the cleaning process into daily manageable steps unlocks the door to efficiency and effectiveness. Rather than viewing bathroom cleaning as a formidable beast to be tackled in one go, dissecting the process into smaller, achievable tasks changes the game. It's like eating a cake; you wouldn't try to swallow it whole. Instead, you take one bite at a time, savoring the process. The same principle applies to cleaning. By dedicating just a few minutes each day to a specific task, you ensure every corner of your bathroom receives the attention it deserves without the overwhelm.

Creating an **actionable and personalized weekly cleaning plan** is the next pivotal step toward maintaining a pristine bathroom. This plan acts as a blueprint, guiding your daily actions and ensuring nothing gets overlooked. It's your roadmap to success, individualized to fit your schedule and cleaning preferences. With a plan in hand, you're equipped to tackle each task methodically, leaving no residue or chaos behind.

Furthermore, **discovering tips for avoiding procrastination and keeping consistent with your cleaning schedule** plays a crucial role in sustaining your success. Consistency is king, and the allure of postponement is the thief that seeks to overthrow your clean kingdom. Combatting this enemy with practical strategies ensures your bathroom remains not just clean, but effortlessly so.

The Step-By-Step Guide to a Glistening Oasis

Step 1: Divide the Cleaning Tasks into Daily Steps

Begin by enumerating all the tasks necessary to maintain a sparkling bathroom. This comprehensive list forms the backbone of your cleaning strategy. Next, break these tasks down into digestible, daily actions. This segmentation transforms an hour-long undertaking into palatable 10-minute increments, making the process less daunting and more man-

42

ageable.

Step 2: Prioritize the Cleaning Tasks

Not all tasks are created equal. Some demand immediate attention for hygienic reasons, such as disinfecting high-touch surfaces and the toilet, while others, like mirror wiping and shower cleaning, elevate the bathroom's aesthetics. Prioritization ensures that your efforts are concentrated where they matter most, balancing necessity with visual appeal.

Step 3: Assign Days and Times for Each Task

With priorities in place, the next step is weaving these tasks into the fabric of your schedule. Identify the days and times when you are most likely to have the energy and uninterrupted minutes to dedicate to cleaning. This personalized timetable becomes your action plan, transforming intention into routine.

Step 4: Gather the Necessary Cleaning Supplies

Before embarking on each task, ensure you have all the required tools at your disposal. This preparatory step not only saves time but also equips you to tackle each cleaning challenge with the right arsenal, ensuring efficiency and effectiveness.

Step 5: Complete Each Task as Scheduled

With preparation complete, it's time to execute your plan. Approach each task with focus, utilizing the proper techniques and products for optimal results. Remember, consistency is key. Adhering to your schedule and completing tasks as planned cultivates a habit of cleanliness, transforming your bathroom into a consistently gleaming sanctuary.

By following these steps, the once overwhelming task of bathroom cleaning becomes a series of manageable actions, each contributing to the overall shine and hygiene of your space. Through discipline, a well-crafted plan, and daily attention, your bathroom can maintain its sparkle, bringing you not just a sense of accomplishment but also the joy of a refreshingly clean retreat.

Master the Art of Breaking Down the Cleaning Process into Daily Manageable Steps

The journey to a consistently clean bathroom doesn't need to be daunting. Imagine trying to drink an entire lake in one gulp - impossible, right? Similarly, attempting to tackle all your bathroom cleaning tasks in one session is not only overwhelming but also impractical. The secret lies in sipping slowly, or in this context, breaking down the cleaning into daily manageable steps. This approach ensures that each task receives the attention it deserves without the entire process becoming a burden.

Every large task, when divided into smaller parts, becomes less intimidating. The bathroom, an area frequented by dust, moisture, and soap scum, requires regular attendance to maintain its sparkle. By dedicating each day to one specific task, such as scrubbing the sink on Monday and cleaning the shower on Tuesday, the cleaning becomes part of your routine rather than an occasional, all-consuming chore. This method also allows for more thorough cleaning since you're focusing on one area at a time.

Think of your cleaning routine as a puzzle. Each piece - or task - needs to fit perfectly to complete the bigger picture, your pristine bathroom. By allocating just a **fifteen-minute window each day** for a different cleaning task, you avoid the pile-up of responsibilities and the dread that comes with a full day of scrubbing and dusting. Remember, the goal is to integrate cleaning into your daily life seamlessly, not to turn it into a dreaded and Herculean task.

Incorporating daily cleaning tasks into your schedule also provides a sense of accomplishment and control. There's something incredibly satisfying about ticking off tasks from a list. It's a visible sign of progress, however small the task may symbolize in the grand scheme of things. This method not only keeps your bathroom continuously clean but also bolsters your motivation to maintain other areas of your home with the same diligence.

Breaking down cleaning tasks into daily steps transforms an overwhelming chore into manageable, bite-sized activities, ensuring thorough attention to every corner of your bathroom.

Create an Actionable and Personalized Weekly Cleaning Plan

Step-by-Step: The Sparkle Cascade System   Step 1: Divide the Cleaning Tasks into Daily Steps

Identify the battleground, the bathroom in this context, and list all the cleaning tasks awaiting your attention. This could range from the mirrors reflecting your weekend decisions to the toilet that's silently pleading for a scrub. Divide these tasks further into ten-minute segments that can fit snugly into your daily routines. For instance, dedicating Monday mornings to rejuvenate the mirrors can add a burst of positivity as you kickstart the week.

Step 2: Prioritize the Cleaning Tasks

Not all tasks weigh the same in the scales of hygiene and aesthetic appeal. Some demand urgency, like banishing harmful germs from your toilet, while others, like ensuring the taps are gleaming, might lean more towards maintaining the bathroom's overall visual appeal. Start with what's crucial for health and hygiene before moving on to tasks that contribute to the bathroom's sparkle and your soul's satisfaction.

Step 3: Assign Days and Times for Each Task

Survey your week - where can these tasks dovetail with your lifestyle without causing disruption? Perhaps Wednesday evening is the perfect time for a shower deep-clean, right before you unwind for the day. Slotting in tasks ensures you're engaging with them at your energy peak, transforming cleaning from a chore into a moment of caretaking for your home and by extension, yourself.

Step 4: Gather the Necessary Cleaning Supplies

A warrior is only as good as their arsenal. Before commencing your scheduled task, assemble your cleaning supplies. This preemptive step prevents time wastage and mental friction, smoothing the path for the task ahead. Knowing your weapons are at hand is half the battle won.

Step 5: Complete Each Task as Scheduled

Adhere to the schedule you've crafted. This focused approach, when coupled with the right techniques and products, promises efficiency and effectiveness in your cleaning routine. If the day's energy ebbs, allow yourself brief intermissions but stay the course. Remember, consistency is key in this endeavor.

These steps, when executed with diligence, construct a robust framework, **The Sparkle Cascade System**, turning an arduous week of cleaning into effortless, daily victories.

Could organizing your tasks with the Sparkle Cascade System be the key to not just a clean bathroom, but a cleaner life?

Discover Tips for Avoiding Procrastination and Keeping Consistent with Your Cleaning Schedule

The war against grime is one fought on two fronts: the physical act of cleaning and the mental battle against procrastination. It's almost magical how the most trivial things become enticing when it's time to clean. Suddenly, rearranging your sock drawer seems like an urgent task. However, with a methodical approach, you can transform cleaning from a dreaded chore into a seamlessly integrated part of your routine.

Imagine if each task you procrastinate on turns into a small gremlin, gnawing away at your peace of mind. The more tasks you push aside, the more populated your space becomes with these invisible stressors. By breaking down your cleaning tasks as suggested in our Sparkle Cascade System, each task completed slays a gremlin, clearing not just physical but also mental clutter.

Step 1: Divide the Cleaning Tasks into Daily Steps

This step is your foundational stone. Small, defined tasks are less intimidating and easily integrated into daily routines, keeping the gremlins at bay.

Step 2: Prioritize the Cleaning Tasks

Tackling high-priority tasks first delivers a significant blow to procrastination. Knowing the essential parts of your bathroom are clean reduces stress and motivates you to handle the less crucial tasks with more vigor.

Step 3: Assign Days and Times for Each Task

A scheduled task is a task half done. Having a specific time allocated for cleaning solidifies your commitment to the task, leaving little room for procrastination.

Step 4: Gather the Necessary Cleaning Supplies

Being prepared is a deterrent to procrastination. If everything you need is within arm's reach, the barrier to begin is significantly lowered.

Step 5: Complete Each Task as Scheduled

Seeing tasks through ensures that procrastination doesn't stand a chance. The satisfaction of completing a task fuels the drive to maintain this momentum throughout your cleaning schedule.

By focusing on one manageable task at a time and celebrating small victories, the mountain of household chores becomes a series of molehills, easily conquered with consistency and dedication.

Integrating cleaning into your daily life through manageable steps, prioritization, and a scheduled approach combats procrastination, fosters consistency, and transforms the bathroom into a continuously refreshed space.

Keep It Simple for Sparkling Results

As you've learned, the key to conquer the cleaning mountain in your bathroom is by breaking it down into small, manageable steps. By focusing on one task at a time, you can ensure that no corner goes unnoticed, ultimately leading to a glistening space that you can be proud of. Remember, **consistency is key**. Setting up a weekly cleaning schedule with specific tasks for each day will help you stay on track and prevent the daunting feeling of having to tackle it all at once.

Take Charge of Your Cleaning Destiny

Don't let procrastination get the best of you. Arm yourself with a solid plan and the determination to stick to it. When you find yourself hesitating or delaying your cleaning tasks, remind yourself of the satisfaction and relief that comes with a sparkling bathroom. **You are in control**, and with each completed task, you're one step closer to a beautifully clean space.

Embrace the Transformation

As you simplify your cleaning routine and establish a consistent schedule, you'll notice a transformation not only in your bathroom but in your mindset as well. The sense of accomplishment that comes with a well-kept space is empowering and can boost your confidence in many areas of your life. **Embrace this journey** towards a cleaner, more organized bathroom, and revel in the sense of pride that comes with it.

6

Germ Warfare: The High-Touch Hotspots

Out of the brisk morning air, Caroline walked into the bathroom with a sense of fierce determination. The news of her youngest child's illness at school struck a chord, echoing past episodes of sickness that plagued her household. Had she been negligent in her cleaning? She questioned herself while her eyes took in the bathroom's familiar terrain, a battleground against invisible foes.

She remembered the pediatrician's words about high-touch areas being the nurseries of germs. Faucets gleamed under the bathroom's fluorescent light. Caroline reached out, her hand pausing mid-air as if the metal spout was hot to the touch. These unassuming fixtures, she thought, as vital as they were everyday, turned sinister in her mind's eye; they were troves of unseen menaces.

Caroline grabbed a rag, dampening it with a mixture of warm water and disinfectant, which filled the air with a sterile pungency. She wiped the faucet's curves and edges, feeling the cool metal become slick under the cleaning agent's influence. Every swipe was a banishment of potential illness, a mother's quiet crusade for her family's well-being. The cloth moved with intent along the doorknob, around its circumference, and over every surface gripped by hands too young to understand the need for such rituals.

As the cloth traversed the landscape of her home's most intimate room, Caroline allowed her thoughts to wade further into the wells of Understanding. The doorknobs took their turn, shining a bit more after their sanitizing shower. Her resolve deepened with the realization that these mundane tasks were acts of preservation, shields in the daily battle for health.

The bathroom door stood ajar, a gust of her children's laughter seeped through the gap from distant rooms. In the juxtaposition of their joy and her vigil, she found a grim sort of beauty. There lay the importance of her endeavor; not just in the eradication of germs, but in the safeguarding of her family's happiness. The simplicity of her action wasn't lost on her, nor was its significance belittled by its routine nature.

What other unassuming daily tasks might carry such weight in the preservation of what we hold dear?

The Hidden Frontline of Germ Warfare

When embarking on the mission to maintain the pristine condition of your bathroom, it's pivotal to zone in on the epicenters of germ activity — the high-touch hotspots. These areas, pervasive yet often overlooked, stand as the primary battlegrounds in the fight against germs. Identifying and sanitizing these regions not only elevates the hygiene of your bathroom but also safeguards the health of your household.

High-touch surfaces in the bathroom, such as faucets, doorknobs, and toilet flush handles, are notorious for harboring germs due to their frequent use. Unwittingly, these surfaces become conduits for the transmission of bacteria and viruses, making them critical areas of focus during your cleaning regimen. It is not merely about wiping these areas down; it involves deploying effective techniques that eradicate pathogens, thereby transforming your bathroom into a sanctuary of cleanliness and health.

50

Learning the art of **sanitizing high-touch areas** effectively does not require sophisticated skills or tools but an understanding of the right methods and products. For instance, while a simple soap and water scrub might suffice for daily upkeep, disinfecting requires targeted solutions that promise to obliterate germs without compromising the integrity of the surfaces. This chapter will guide you through selecting appropriate disinfectants and mastering the techniques to ensure these hotspots remain not just visually clean but hygienically safe.

Moreover, **regular disinfection** of these high-touch surfaces emerges as a non-negotiable practice in the crusade against germ spread. It's a habit that when cultivated, significantly reduces the likelihood of pathogen transmission within your home. This chapter will illuminate the frequency and methodology of disinfection that aligns with the goal of maintaining a hygienic bathroom environment.

Understanding the *why* behind focusing on these high-touch areas unravels the relationship between regular household cleaning and the promotion of health. It transcends the quest for a visually appealing bathroom to underscore the role of cleanliness in fortifying the wellbeing of your living space. This insight fosters a profound appreciation for the meticulous attention to these germ hotspots, elevating your cleaning routine from a chore to a protective measure for your home.

Through practical advice and insightful guidance, this chapter endeavors to empower you with the knowledge and tools to effectively combat the germs lurking in your bathroom. As you turn each page, envision yourself not just as someone cleaning a bathroom but as a guardian of health, armed with the prowess to tackle germs where they thrive most ferociously. Welcome to the frontline of germ warfare, where your efforts in addressing these high-touch areas impart a lasting impact on the cleanliness and health of your bathroom and beyond.

Identifying Germ Havens in Your Bathroom

In the realm of bathroom cleanliness, certain areas act as bustling metropolises for germs, thriving unseen to the naked eye. These high-touch zones, such as faucets, doorknobs, and even the humble toilet flush, are akin to the doorways of our daily routines. Just as a doormat collects the debris of countless steps, these areas gather the microscopic remnants of our day, harboring bacteria and viruses in silent anonymity.

A study by the National Sanitation Foundation (NSF) found that faucets, in particular, are hotbeds for germ activity. Faucets are not only touched frequently throughout the day but also offer a moist environment where germs can multiply rapidly. Light switches and door handles follow closely, acting as conduits for germs to spread from person to person within a household.

Imagine if these high-touch areas were like sponges in a kitchen sink, absorbing everything they encounter. Just as a sponge can spread the contaminants it picks up to other surfaces, so too can these bathroom fixtures spread germs to our hands - and subsequently to our faces and other parts of the home. This analogy highlights the importance of not only identifying but also prioritizing these areas during cleaning to minimize health risks.

Moreover, the toilet handle, often overlooked, is a prime example of a germ harbor. Despite its essential function, it's frequently forgotten in the cleaning routine, allowing germs to build up and spread with each flush. Alongside, shared items like towels and toothbrush holders also play a significant role in germ transmission, emphasizing the need for their regular cleaning.

In confronting the hidden dangers of high-touch areas in our bathrooms, awareness is the first step to prevention. By targeting these germ hotspots, we can significantly reduce the spread of harmful bacteria and viruses, ensuring a healthier living environment.

The key point is to identify and prioritize cleaning

faucets, doorknobs, toilet handles, and other high-touch areas to reduce the spread of germs.

Sanitizing with Precision

The act of sanitizing these germ-laden zones is akin to wielding a shield in battle, a primary defense mechanism against the unseen enemy lurking on surfaces. Effective sanitization involves not just a cursory wipe but a thorough cleansing that ensures these microscopic adversaries are rendered harmless.

For faucets and doorknobs, the Centers for Disease Control and Prevention (CDC) recommends a two-step process: cleaning followed by disinfecting. Cleaning involves the removal of dirt and impurities from surfaces, which in itself can reduce the number of germs. However, disinfecting goes a step further by using chemicals to kill the germs on surfaces. This one-two punch is essential for breaking the chain of infection in our homes.

One popular technique involves the use of diluted household bleach solutions, alcohol solutions with at least 70% alcohol, and EPA-registered household disinfectants. It's critical to ensure the product is suited for the surface to avoid damage. For an added layer of protection, wear disposable gloves and ensure good ventilation during the cleaning process.

Imagine sanitizing as polishing a diamond; it's not merely about making it look clean but ensuring its brilliance by meticulously removing all that dims its sparkle. Similarly, sanitizing high-touch bathroom areas requires both attention to detail and the right tools to ensure we're not just displacing germs but effectively neutralizing them.

For those concerned about harsh chemicals, natural alternatives like vinegar and hydrogen peroxide offer a gentler approach, although their effectiveness varies. Regardless of the method, the key is consistency and thoroughness, ensuring no nook or cranny is left unattended.

Now, envision a routine where sanitizing these hotspots

becomes second nature, seamlessly integrated into our daily lives. This not only promotes a healthier living environment but also instills a sense of well-being and assurance.

Could this simple change in our cleaning habits be the shield that guards our health against the invisible threats?

The Pillar of Regular Disinfection

Maintaining a pristine bathroom goes beyond aesthetics; it's about fostering a sanctuary of health and hygiene. Regular disinfection stands as a cornerstone in this endeavor, embodying the proactive measures necessary to thwart the proliferation of germs.

Consider the bathroom not just as a space for personal hygiene but as a living ecosystem where germs can thrive if left unchecked. Like gardeners who cultivate their soil and prune their plants to prevent disease, we too must tend to this environment with regular care and vigilance. This analogy underscores the importance of disinfection as an ongoing commitment rather than a sporadic effort.

The frequency of this ritual plays a crucial role. High-touch surfaces, due to their constant use, necessitate daily attention to effectively curtail the germ population. This routine does not have to be laborious; with the right tools and techniques, it can be woven seamlessly into our daily lives, much like brushing our teeth or making our beds.

Incorporating regular disinfection into our routines instills a disciplined approach to hygiene, transforming what can seem like a tedious chore into a beneficial habit. This not only ensures the cleanliness of our bathrooms but also contributes to the well-being of our households by safeguarding against the spread of illness.

A regular schedule, consistent products, and a methodical approach lay the groundwork for effective disinfection, serving as our steady hand in the ongoing care of our spaces. This regimen not only combats germs but also reinforces a mindset of mindfulness and responsibility toward our environment.

By identifying high-touch germ hotspots, master-ing effective sanitization techniques, and committing to regular disinfection, we fortify our homes against unseen threats, ensuring a sanctuary of cleanliness and health.

A Fresh Start for a Germ-Free Bathroom

As we wrap up our discussion on germ warfare in your bath-room, it's clear that **high-touch areas are the breeding grounds for harmful bacteria.** By identifying these spots and learning how to effectively sanitize them, you're taking a crucial step towards a cleaner and healthier bathroom en-vironment. Remember, **regular disinfection is key to maintaining a hygienic space** that sparkles with clean-liness.

Keeping Germs at Bay

Now that you're equipped with the knowledge of which ar-eas to target and how to clean them effectively, it's time to put that knowledge into action. **Prioritize cleaning high-touch areas like faucets and doorknobs** during each cleaning session to ensure that these commonly used spots are free from germs. By focusing on these key locations, you're not only preventing the spread of bacteria but also creating a safer space for yourself and your loved ones.

Transforming Your Bathroom Routine

By integrating these cleaning techniques into your regular bathroom maintenance, you're not just cleaning – you're **pro-tecting your health.** Think of it as a small investment in your well-being that will pay off in the long run. With each wipe and scrub, you're not only removing dirt and grime but also eradicating harmful germs that could potentially cause illness. **Consistency is key**, so keep up the good work to enjoy a sparkling and germ-free bathroom.

Step into a Cleaner Tomorrow

As you continue on your cleaning journey, remember that a sparkling bathroom isn't just about appearances – it's about creating a healthy and inviting space for yourself and others. So, don't underestimate the power of tackling those high-touch hotspots. Embrace the process, maintain a regular cleaning schedule, and revel in the fresh, clean atmosphere you've worked so hard to achieve. **Your bathroom is your sanctuary – let it sparkle and shine with confidence.**

7

Surface Success: Tailor Your Tactic

The sun was already high and unforgiving as Martin wiped the sweat from his brow with the back of his hand. He stood in the doorway of the small bathroom, his eyes scrutinizing every surface with a critical gaze. From the glass shower enclosure speckled with water spots to the tile peppered with grimy grout, every inch summoned the resolve for a deep, rejuvenating cleanse.

Martin's mind raced with memories of dull porcelain and streaked mirrors, relics of his past attempts that had left surfaces marred rather than meticulously cleaned. He inhaled deeply, the sharp scent of chlorine-tinged cleaners reminding him of the task at hand. The mop rested in the corner, its handle like a silent observer to the ritual that was about to begin.

As he dampened the sponge, his thoughts wandered to the elegance of the tile when first laid—a seascape of blue and white that had brightened the entire room. He pictured how it must have felt underfoot, cool and smooth, leading one willingly into the embrace of a warm bath. His hands moved with purpose, caressing the tile with a cleaner specially selected for its gentle effectiveness. The grout, that tricky custodian of tile's beauty, called for a small brush, its bristles firm yet careful not to gouge or scrape.

His movement paused momentarily as he caught sight of his reflection in the shower door—a canvas besmirched by droplets turned into calcified blemishes. With a soft cloth in hand, he approached the glass as one might a delicate piece of art. His motions were steady and deliberate, the product he had chosen promised to respect the fragility of that transparent barrier. It was a dance of sorts—spray, wipe, and buff—a rhythm gleaned from past missteps where too much pressure or the wrong chemical concoction would leave behind more than just the memory of water.

Lastly, his gaze fell upon the porcelain throne, a fixture so often taken for granted in its pristine whiteness when cared for, but so quickly reduced to an object of scorn when neglected. He selected a non-abrasive cleaner, one that would treat the porcelain with the adoration it deserved, ensuring it would not suffer from the abrasive scrubs of yesteryear.

With each stroke, each repetitive motion, Martin was not just cleaning; he was restoring—a silent penance for past oversights. Once done, he stood back to admire his work: glass shimmered with renewed clarity, tile and grout formed a harmonious patchwork free of filth, and porcelain gleamed, almost proudly, under the fluorescent light.

As the day drew to a close and shadows lengthened across the freshly-laundered floors, Martin couldn't help but dwell on the transformation. Was it the bathroom that had been restored, or was it something within him, a satisfaction drawn from mastery over these stubborn surfaces? And as he thought about the work of his hands, he wondered whether his techniques were as refined as they could be—what hidden secrets to surface preservation lay out there, waiting to be discovered?

A Gleaming Start: Tailoring Your Tactic to Every Surface

Embarking on a journey to achieve a sparkling clean bathroom is not just about putting in the effort; it's about applying the right techniques to the right places. Every surface in your bathroom, be it glass, tile, grout, or porcelain, demands a unique approach. This understanding is crucial if you want to prevent damage and ensure that not only are your cleaning efforts effective but that they also contribute to the longevity and aesthetic appeal of your bathroom fixtures. It's time to dive deep into discovering the secrets to mastering these techniques, ensuring your bathroom not only sparkles but also reflects your commitment to maintaining its shine and health.

The **first crucial step** is to recognize that not all surfaces are created equal. This differentiation is fundamental in the realm of bathroom cleaning. Identifying the materials you're dealing with and their specific needs is as essential as selecting the right product off a shelf. Just as you wouldn't use sandpaper to clean a mirror, harsh chemicals or the wrong scrubbing tools can cause irreversible damage to sensitive surfaces.

Moving forward, **knowing the exact requirements** for each type of surface is your blueprint to success. For instance, the delicate dance of cleaning glass involves ensuring streak-free results without leaving behind any residue that could attract more dirt. On the other hand, tackling the roughness of tile and the nuances of grout requires a gentle yet effective approach to remove grime without compromising the integrity of these surfaces.

However, knowledge alone isn't power unless applied correctly. A common pitfall in bathroom maintenance is the **misapplication of techniques and products**. Using abrasive substances on delicate surfaces or employing excessive force can do more harm than good. It's not just about what you clean but how you clean it. Understanding and avoiding these common mistakes can save you from the pain of seeing your cherished bathroom lose its luster.

The Sparkle Steps: Your Path to Perfection

Step 1: Identify the Different Bathroom Surfaces Take a quick tour of your bathroom, making a mental note of the materials present. This first step should take no more than a few minutes but forms the bedrock of your cleaning strategy. Each material has its quirks and requires a tailored approach for the best results.

Step 2: Know the Cleaning Needs and Techniques for Each Surface Dedicate some time to research or consult this guide on the specific dos and don'ts for each surface type. Glass, for instance, prefers a gentle touch with a non-abrasive cleaner, while tile and grout may welcome a bit of elbow grease with more forgiving substances. Expect to invest about an hour in this learning process, ensuring you're well-armed with knowledge.

Step 3: Avoid Common Cleaning Mistakes Awareness of what not to do is as vital as knowing the right steps. Spend about 30 minutes understanding the common missteps, like using vinegary solutions on stone tiles, which can etch the surface. These insights are pivotal in safeguarding your bathroom's aesthetics and integrity.

Step 4: Select the Best Products and Tools Choosing the right arsenal of cleaning products and tools doesn't have to be daunting. Allow yourself about 45 minutes to conduct research, favoring products that are highly recommended for your specific surface types. Factors such as effectiveness, environmental friendliness, and ease of use should guide your selection.

Step 5: Follow the Recommended Cleaning Methods

With all the knowledge and tools at your disposal, it's time to put theory into practice. Each surface, with its unique care instructions, demands attention to detail. For glass, embrace a gentle circular motion; for tiles and grout, a bit more vigor may be necessary. Allocate sufficient time for each cleaning session—rushing can lead to oversight and potential damage.

Each step, meticulously followed, transforms the cleaning process from a mundane chore into a rewarding journey towards maintaining the beauty and longevity of your bathroom. It's a testament to the power of knowledge, technique, and the right tools in achieving results that don't just clean the surface but enhance the overall health and brilliance of your bathroom fixtures. Through these steps, your path to a gleaming bathroom becomes not just a possibility, but a reality.

Understanding Bathroom Surfaces: A Dip into Diverse Needs

Every surface in your bathroom from the tile floors to the porcelain throne, holds a story written in splashes, soap scum, and sometimes, the unfortunate lime scale. These stories, while unique, share a common need—a cleaning approach that respects their nature. **Tiles**, being quite porous, can harbor germs in their nooks and crannies, requiring a gentle but effective cleansing regiment. **Grout**, the unsung hero holding your tiles in place, demands attention too, often needing a touch of baking soda magic to stay pristine.

Imagine your bathroom as a garden. Each plant – or in this case, surface – thrives with different care; glass shines under a gentle mist while porcelain demands a sturdier hand. **Glass surfaces** in your bathroom, for instance, hate to be streaked and smeared, preferring the soft caress of a lint-free cloth paired with a loving spray of a glass cleaner. **Porcelain**, on the other hand, is robust and forgiving, but it still despises harsh chemicals that can etch its glossy finish.

Understanding these requirements isn't just about keeping appearances; it's about preserving the life and luster of your bathroom fixtures. Over time, the wrong cleaning method can dull the sparkle you're working so hard to achieve, turning your retreat into a place of retreat for everything but cleanliness.

In a dance of sponges, cloths, and cleaners, each step, each movement, needs to be adjusted to the music played by each surface. The tile might enjoy a brisk tango of gentle abrasives and soft cloths, while the delicate waltz of glass cleaner and duster suits the mirror best.

In mastering the art of cleaning, it is pivotal to understand the unique language each surface speaks, ensuring their gleaming testimonies to your home's hygiene and care.

Surface Smarts: Avoiding the Pitfalls of Cleaning

Identify the Different Bathroom Surfaces

Taking a moment to survey your bathroom is the first step towards a tailored cleaning regime. Identify the players—the glass making your mirrors, the tiles underfoot, the grout peeking between them, and the porcelain of your sink and toilet. Each of these materials comes with its own set of cleaning specifications, implicitly asking for the right approach to ensure they stay in top form.

Know the Cleaning Needs and Techniques for Each Surface

Next, dive into the specific needs and techniques required for each identified surface. This step is akin to crafting a bespoke suit—every measurement is crucial for the perfect fit. For glass, a concoction that leaves no streaks behind is essential, while tile and grout might invite a more hands-on approach with a scrub and a homemade cleaner of baking soda and water.

Avoid Common Cleaning Mistakes

Awareness of the pitfalls in cleaning these surfaces is akin to knowing the roads to avoid during rush hour—it saves you time and preserves your sanity. Hard lessons remind us that abrasive cleaners can leave permanent marks on delicate surfaces, and that overzealous scrubbing can do more harm than good, especially to the integrity of something as crucial as grout.

Select the Best Products and Tools

The choice of cleaning products and tools is not unlike selecting the right outfit for an occasion—what works for a casual outing won't necessarily suit a formal event. The effectiveness, safety, and ease of use of these products are paramount, guiding you towards those that have garnered positive reviews and shown to be champions for specific surfaces.

Follow the Recommended Cleaning Methods

Embarking on the actual cleaning process, it's important to apply what you've learned. Spray and wipe glass surfaces with care, scrub tile and grout with the precision of an artist, and always, always, follow the set guidelines for each cleaning method. It's in this careful following of instructions that you achieve the results you desire, making your bathroom a gleaming testament to your efforts.

Could considering each surface's needs and adopting tailored cleaning techniques be the secret to maintaining a spotless and durable bathroom?

The Arsenal of Cleanliness: Equip Yourself Right

To embark on your cleaning mission, a well-stocked arsenal is essential. Not just any cleaning agent or tool will do; specificity is your ally in this battle against grime.

Identify the Different Bathroom Surfaces

The journey begins with reconnaissance—mapping out the terrain of your bathroom. Each surface, whether it be the reflective mirage of glass, the textured landscape of tile, or the smooth plains of porcelain, has its ally in the cleaning world, chosen for its ability to enhance rather than diminish.

Know the Cleaning Needs and Techniques for Each Surface

Consider each surface a distinct ecosystem within the larger environment of your bathroom. Like a gardener who knows that roses thrive with certain nutrients while cacti demand another set entirely, so must you recognize the individual needs of glass, tile, grout, and porcelain. From gentle spritzes to robust scrubs, each method is a tailored touch meant to preserve the surface's integrity while restoring its shine.

Avoid Common Cleaning Mistakes

Wielding this knowledge shields your bathroom's ecosystems from the blight of common cleaning missteps—harsh chemicals on delicate surfaces, overzealous scrubbing on grout, and the like. This insight serves as the guardian of their longevity and beauty, ensuring that each swipe, spray, and scrub is a step towards revitalization, not deterioration.

Select the Best Products and Tools

Choosing your tools and agents for this task is much like curating a gallery show; each item selected for its contribution to the overall aesthetic. Effectiveness, safety, ease of use—these are your criteria, guiding you to the products that promise not just cleanliness but care for each specific surface.

Follow the Recommended Cleaning Methods

Armed and informed, you engage in the art of cleaning with precision and respect for the materials under your care. Like a sculptor who knows just how to chisel marble to avoid cracks, your methods are gentle yet effective, ensuring each surface is treated with the reverence it demands.

Understanding the unique cleaning needs of each bathroom surface, avoiding common pitfalls with informed technique, and selecting the right products

and tools—these are the cornerstone practices that ensure a gleaming, well-preserved bathroom.

Recap of Essential Tips for Surface Cleaning Success

Mastering effective cleaning techniques for different surfaces is crucial to avoid damage and ensure your bathroom dazzles with cleanliness. By understanding the specific needs of surfaces like glass, tile, grout, and porcelain, you can achieve optimal cleaning results and prolong the life of your bathroom fixtures.

Embrace Tailored Cleaning Techniques

Understanding the specific cleaning needs of each surface is key. From the gentle touch required for glass to the scrubbing power needed for grout, tailoring your cleaning approach is essential. Use the right tools and products for each surface to achieve the best results without causing harm.

Avoid common mistakes that can damage surfaces. By steering clear of abrasive cleaners on delicate surfaces and using soft cloths or sponges instead of harsh scrubbers, you'll protect your bathroom fixtures from unnecessary wear and tear.

Invest in quality products and tools. From microfiber cloths for glass to grout brushes for those hard-to-reach areas, having the right equipment at your disposal will make your cleaning tasks more efficient and effective.

Achieve Sparkling Results Every Time

Adapt your cleaning strategy to suit the surface at hand. Different surfaces require different techniques, so be sure to adjust your approach accordingly. For example, a gentle wipe-down might work wonders on glass, whereas tile and grout may need a more vigorous scrubbing.

Consistency is key. Regular maintenance and cleaning routines tailored to each surface type will keep your bathroom looking its best and prevent the need for deep cleaning sessions down the line.

Remember, knowledge is power. The more you understand about the surfaces in your bathroom, the better equipped you'll be to keep them looking their finest. By mastering the art of cleaning tailored to different surfaces, you'll ensure your bathroom shines with long-lasting beauty.

8

Order in the Court: Organizing Your Cleaning Supplies

The sun cascaded its morning glory into the cramped confines of Mary's suburban kitchen, where the scent of lemon polish had long settled into the fabric of the curtains. She stood there, the chaos of bottles and rags unconquered before her. The cabinet under the sink—a fiercely defended territory of soaps and solvents—was a battleground of disorder. The bottles jostled for supremacy, while sponges and brushes lay slain in the shadows. She sighed.

In the cacophony of the clinking glass and the rustling of plastic, there was a momentary pause as Mary, with purpose, pulled the entire contents of the cabinet onto the kitchen floor. She felt a pang of nostalgia as she picked up an old, weary mop that had danced through countless spills and mishaps. Its once pristine strands were now matted with the history of ground-in grime and dust bunnies. It was time, she knew, for this trusty ally to retire.

As she sorted through the graveyard of half-used products, the memory of her mother's immaculate house whispered to her. There, everything had its place. A home within a home, her mother would say, where no sponge was left to wonder of its purpose, no bottle misplaced. It was this memory that spurred Mary to seek order in her own chaotic corner of the world. For how could she embody the calm her mother had always instilled if her tools of tranquility were in disarray?

She decided then and there. She would carve out a sanctuary for her army of cleaners. A sturdy shelf in the garage, perhaps—a throne for the solutions that washed away the toils of daily living. Or a simple caddy that could venture room to room, always prepared, a sentinel against the never-ending tide of spills and stains. With each spray bottle and scouring pad finding its rightful place, Mary felt a symphony of order begin to play, each note a promise of easier days to come.

Mary juggled the responsibilities of her day—calls to be made, errands to run—but the project at hand was her anchor. She knew the time invested now would unfurl countless hours in the future. She deliberated on the inventories of her mother's pantry and made a mental list of what to replenish, what to release back into the wilds of the retail jungle. Through maintaining a careful balance, she would ensure that no urgent cleaning crisis would catch her unprepared.

With the sun now high, imparting a warmth that spoke of the afternoon to come, Mary paused to wipe a brow beaded with the honest sweat of manual toil. She surveyed the fruits of her labor, seeing not just the sparkling surface of tamed domesticity, but perhaps, a reflection of her mother's knowing smile. What victories could be won with the right tools in their proper place, and what peace could be found in the rhythms of care and maintenance? Might the song of order that now swelled in her heart be the prelude to a dance of ease and predictability?

Unlock the Secret to Effortless Cleaning

Imagine stepping into your bathroom to find it not only sparkling clean but also incredibly inviting, all because you've mastered the art of organization. This goes beyond the usual tidying up; it's about turning your cleaning supply closet into a powerhouse of efficiency. In the bustling world we live in, the last thing anyone needs is to fumble through a chaotic stash of bottles, sponges, and whatnot. That's precisely why dedicating a space for your cleaning supplies can revolutionize the way you approach bathroom maintenance.

Having a designated area for your cleaning supplies is not just about neatness; it's about adding speed and effectiveness to your cleaning routine. When every scrub, spray, and cloth has its own spot, you eliminate the time spent searching for supplies, allowing you to dive straight into the task. This simple yet crucial organization step ensures that maintaining a glistening bathroom becomes less of a chore and more of a swift, satisfying accomplishment.

Discovering organizational tips and storage solutions for your cleaning arsenal is akin to unlocking a new level in a game. It's about finding the perfect balance between accessibility and aesthetics. Shelf organizers, under-sink caddies, and labeled bins can transform a cluttered space into an orderly haven. These tools not only make it easier to grab what you need but also protect your supplies from damage and ensure that everything is in excellent condition for when duty calls.

Maintaining an inventory and efficiently restocking your cleaning supplies can, surprisingly, be quite gratifying. *Knowing exactly what you have and what you need to replenish can save you time, money, and unnecessary stress.* A simple checklist or a digital inventory can serve as a reminder to replace products before they run out, ensuring you're always prepared for a cleaning session. This proactive approach not only keeps your bathroom shining but also alleviates the hassle of last-minute runs to the store.

Streamline Your Cleaning Process

The transformation begins with decluttering. By removing expired or unnecessary items, you create more room for the essentials. This step is crucial in building a foundation for an organized space where each item is easily accessible. It's about making smart choices and understanding that less is often more when it comes to efficient cleaning.

Implementing a system that works for you is key. Whether it's arranging products by use frequency or grouping them by type, the goal is to reduce the time spent searching for supplies. Simple changes, such as installing hooks for hanging items or using clear containers for visibility, can make a significant impact on your daily routine.

Keeping your cleaning supplies organized might seem like a small part of overall home maintenance, but its impact can be profound. Just as a well-oiled machine performs better, a well-organized cleaning supply closet can significantly enhance your cleaning efficiency. This practice not only saves time but also encourages a more frequent and thus more effective cleaning routine. After all, when the tools of the trade are right at your fingertips, embarking on a cleaning spree becomes less daunting and more approachable.

In the grand scheme of things, embracing these organizational habits promises not just a cleaner space but also a smoother, more enjoyable cleaning experience. It's about setting yourself up for success from the get-go and relishing the seamless flow of your cleaning routine. With everything in its right place, you're not just cleaning; you're creating a sanctuary that reflects the effort and care you invest in your home. And there's truly nothing more rewarding than that.

Exploring the Benefits of Having a Designated Area for Your Cleaning Supplies

Imagine walking into your kitchen to start your daily cleaning routine. You reach under the sink, and without shuffling through a jumbled mess of bottles and sponges, you instantly

70

grab what you need. This isn't just a dream; it's the reality for those who have discovered the benefits of having a designated area for their cleaning supplies. Keeping cleaning products in a specific spot creates a streamlined process, minimizing the time and effort spent on what many see as a chore.

Having everything in its place isn't just about tidiness; it's about efficiency. When you know exactly where your cleaning supplies are, you don't waste time looking for them. This efficiency can reduce the dread associated with cleaning and turn it into a more manageable, even enjoyable, task. Like a well-organized toolbox for a mechanic, having a designated storage area for cleaning supplies equips you with the means for a job well done, without the added frustration of rummaging through a cluttered cabinet.

Another essential benefit is safety. Storing cleaning supplies in one area, preferably out of reach of children and pets, reduces the risk of accidents. Certain cleaning agents, if mixed inadvertently, can create harmful fumes or reactions. A designated storage space helps prevent such dangers, ensuring that only the right products are used together safely. It's akin to keeping all medicines in one cabinet, securely out of harm's way - a simple yet effective practice to safeguard the household.

Moreover, a well-organized cleaning supply storage can save you money. When you can see all your cleaning products at a glance, you're less likely to buy duplicates of items you already have but couldn't find. This visibility not only helps in making more informed purchasing decisions but also in using products more effectively, ensuring that nothing goes to waste.

Keeping your cleaning supplies in a designated area streamlines your cleaning routine, enhances safety, and saves money.

Discover Organizational Tips and Storage Solutions for Cleaning Products and Tools

Finding the right organizational tips and storage solutions for your cleaning supplies can be likened to creating a personalized cookbook for your home care routine. Each home is unique, offering different challenges and spaces for storage. The goal is to tailor your approach, turning chaotic cabinets and overstuffed drawers into models of efficiency.

Start by decluttering. Evaluate your cleaning supplies, discarding expired products and those you no longer use. This step is crucial, akin to pruning a garden: it allows for new growth and makes space for what truly matters. Once you've pared down to the essentials, consider how often you use each item. Daily-use products should be most accessible, while less frequently used items can be stored higher up or in more remote parts of your storage space.

A variety of storage solutions can elevate your organizational game. Over-the-door organizers, for example, can transform an unused space into a tidy storage area for bottles and tools. Clear storage bins are another versatile option, allowing you to see what's inside without opening them. These solutions don't just organize; they reveal. Like clear labels on a spice rack, they help you quickly identify and reach for exactly what you need.

Think vertically to maximize space. Shelving units, whether freestanding or mounted on the wall, can dramatically increase your storage area without taking up precious floor space. This strategy is particularly useful in smaller homes or apartments where every inch counts. Imagine stacking your cleaning supplies like a carefully constructed tower of blocks, with each level easily accessible and in sight.

Reflect on the connections between your cleaning habits and the space you inhabit. Could rearranging your supplies not just declutter your cabinets, but also declutter your mind, making the daunting task of cleaning a more serene and manageable aspect of your daily life? Utilizing the right storage solutions and organizational tips can transform your cleaning routine into an efficient and even enjoyable process.

Could finding joy in the organization of your cleaning supplies be the key to transforming the chore of cleaning into an act of care for your home and yourself?

Understand How to Maintain an Inventory and Restock Your Cleaning Supplies Efficiently

Keeping an inventory of your cleaning supplies sounds like a task fit for a retail manager, but it's a simple and effective strategy that any homeowner can implement. By knowing what you have, you can avoid the frustration of running out of your favorite bathroom cleaner right before guests arrive or purchasing a third bottle of window cleaner because you forgot the other two were hiding behind larger items. This approach is about creating a system, much like a library organizes its books, ensuring you can always find what you need when you need it.

Begin with a straightforward inventory list, noting what products you have and their quantities. This list can be as simple as a handwritten note or as sophisticated as a digital spreadsheet, whatever works best for you. Update it whenever you use up or buy new cleaning supplies. The goal here is not to become bogged down in details but to have a clear overview of your cleaning arsenal at any given time.

Restocking efficiently goes hand in hand with maintaining an inventory. Keep an eye on your supplies, making a habit of checking your stock before it dips too low. This preemptive approach is akin to watering plants before they wilt, keeping everything vibrant and usable. Also, consider buying in bulk items you use frequently, which can save money and reduce the number of shopping trips. However, balance is key. Buying too much can lead to clutter, defeating the purpose of organizing your supplies.

By maintaining an inventory and restocking efficiently,

you not only ensure that your cleaning routine remains uninterrupted by unexpected shortages but also make your purchasing more mindful and economical. This method takes the guesswork out of shopping for cleaning supplies, allowing you to focus on what truly matters: keeping your home sparkling clean with minimal stress.

Organizing your cleaning supplies, discovering storage solutions, and efficiently maintaining an inventory not only streamlines your cleaning process but transforms it into an act of care for your home.

Final Thoughts

By setting up a designated area for your cleaning supplies, you're not just tidying up your space – you're setting yourself up for success. **Organizing your cleaning products not only saves you time but also eliminates unnecessary stress** when it's time to refresh your bathroom.

Stay Ahead of the Game

Remember, **a well-organized cleaning supply station can be a game-changer in your cleaning routine.** Make use of baskets, shelves, or cabinets to keep your products sorted and accessible. Investing a little time now in arranging your supplies will pay off in the long run with smoother, stress-free cleaning sessions.

Stock Smartly

Setting up a system for **tracking your cleaning supplies inventory will ensure you never run out of essential products when you need them.** Create a list or use a simple spreadsheet to note down what you have and what you're running low on. This proactive approach will save you from last-minute trips to the store in the middle of a cleaning spree.

Next Steps

Now that you've learned the benefits of organization, **put these practical tips into action to transform your cleaning routine.** Designate a space, get creative with storage solutions, and keep track of your inventory. By doing so, you'll streamline your cleaning process, making it a breeze to maintain a sparkling, fresh bathroom.

9

The Proactive Path: Keep It Clean Without a Fuss

Amidst the serene chaos of early morning, the sunlight dribbled through the slats of Linda's bathroom window, casting long, slender shadows over the ceramic tiles that lay cold beneath her bare feet. Her gaze roamed the room, landing on the half-empty tubes of toothpaste disgracing the rim of the sink, towels in repose on the floor like weary travelers, and a shower curtain grimy with the residues of hurried mornings. A sigh escaped her as she reminded herself, "This place is a sanctuary, not a cell."

She had read somewhere, perhaps in a discarded magazine at the doctor's office, about the art of maintaining a clean bathroom with minimal effort. The concept was simple, but it seemed to slip through her fingers like the water that went down the plughole each morning. It whispered promises of gleaming surfaces that never knew the indignity of a water stain, and a reflected face never framed by the fog of accumulated grime. It was this very morning that a resolve had wormed its way into her consciousness, setting roots in the fertile ground of discontent.

A grim tableau, her bathroom had become a stage for daily acts of neglect, each abandoned towel and each streak on the mirror a testament to postponed responsibility. Linda, tender-footed, stepped around the clutter, plucking a stray sock from the tile, an artifact of the night before. As she stooped, her back protested, a subtle reminder of her age. There was a pang of guilt, too, for letting things slide, for allowing the creeping tide of disorder to claim another space in her home.

As she straightened the bathmat with a gentle tug, her thoughts tumbled to strategies of empowerment. She envisioned a schedule, tucked on the back of the door – a blueprint, showing when to scrub, when to sweep, when to savor the sanctity of cleanliness. She fancied investing in baskets and shelves that could act as bastions against the relentless advance of chaos. Yet, were these not just beautiful battles in a war she felt too tired to wage?

A small hand interrupted her reverie, pressing into hers— it was her daughter, home early from a sleepover, her raven curls tangled like the thoughts in Linda's head. "Mommy, can I take a bath?" she chirped, oblivious to the disorder. Linda knelt, drawing her daughter into a tight embrace, the warmth of her small body melting some of the frost in her own resolve. She whispered a 'yes', pecked her on the forehead, and watched as the little one shed her nightie with a flourish and stepped into the tub, creating soft ripples in the calm water.

Could Linda find harmony between the sanctity of family life and the tyranny of the tidy? The bathroom, a silent witness to the patterns of their lives, seemed to hold its breath, waiting for her surrender—or salvation. Could the simplicity of a thought—a foresight, a plan—tame the everyday beast of disarray? If so, might it not echo through the rest of her home, her life?

Master the Art of Proactive Cleaning

The secret to maintaining a sparkling bathroom without turning it into an overwhelming project lies in embracing a proactive approach to cleaning. This mindset shift—where you address messes as they occur rather than letting them build up—is not just about keeping your bathroom looking good; it's about creating a space that reflects the calm and order we all seek in our lives. By developing proactive cleaning habits, you unlock the first key lesson in maintaining bathroom cleanliness with ease.

Imagine walking into your bathroom not to be met with dread over the cleaning that awaits but with peace, knowing that everything is already in its place and shining brightly. This mental image is achievable and, believe it or not, with much less effort than you might think. The trick? **Learning strategies for staying on top of bathroom maintenance tasks** with minimal effort. This involves creating a simple, yet effective, routine that slots seamlessly into your daily life, preventing the dreaded buildup of grime and clutter.

Now, you might be wondering how to make this dream a reality. Understanding how to implement organizational systems that support ongoing cleanliness is our third crucial lesson. Organizing your cleaning supplies, toiletries, and linens in an accessible and logical manner is not just about aesthetics; it's about functionality. When every item has a home, and you can easily access your cleaning tools, the task of cleaning becomes less of a chore and more of a straightforward, quick activity.

Let's not underestimate the power of a schedule. By **following a schedule**, you're not only ensuring consistent cleanliness, but you're also setting yourself up for success. This doesn't mean dedicating entire afternoons to scrubbing and polishing but integrating small, manageable tasks into your daily routine. The beauty of a proactive cleaning schedule is that it allows you to spread out the workload, making cleaning feel like less of a job and more like a simple habit.

Remember, the goal is not perfection but progress. Beginning your journey towards a consistently clean bathroom can seem daunting, but patience and persistence are your best allies. Celebrate the small victories—a streak-free mirror, a clutter-free countertop—and know that with each step, you're creating a more inviting space.

The Tools and Systems That Speak to Success

Achieving a constantly clean bathroom is less about the time spent cleaning and more about the efficiency and effectiveness of the methods and tools used. Investing in the right cleaning supplies that make the job easier and more enjoyable is a step often overlooked. From microfiber cloths that trap dust and dirt to eco-friendly cleaning solutions that are tough on grime but gentle on surfaces, choosing the right tools can make a significant difference.

An organizational system that complements your lifestyle and the layout of your bathroom plays a vital role in maintaining cleanliness. This could be as simple as having a designated storage area for cleaning supplies or implementing a "use it or lose it" policy to keep clutter at bay. The key is to find a system that works for you—one that is easy to follow and helps keep your cleaning schedule on track.

Adopting a proactive approach to cleaning your bathroom may require a shift in mindset and some initial setup, but the payoff is a consistently clean and inviting space. By developing proactive cleaning habits, learning strategies to stay on top of maintenance tasks, and implementing organizational systems, you embrace a foolproof method that not only transforms your bathroom but also enhances your overall quality of life.ediator

Developing Proactive Cleaning Habits

To keep a bathroom sparkling without breaking a sweat involves deploying a set of proactive cleaning habits. Essentially, this means addressing messes and dirt *as soon as they happen.* Imagine your bathroom as a living organism that needs regular care to stay healthy. Just as you wouldn't let a small wound fester because it could lead to further infection, treating your bathroom to immediate attention when spills, smudges, or any mess occurs preserves its cleanliness and prevents the task from becoming overwhelmingly large later on.

In the realm of efficient bathroom maintenance, prevention is key. For instance, wiping down the shower walls after each use with a squeegee can significantly reduce mold and mildew buildup, which, if left unattended, requires more rigorous and abrasive cleaning solutions down the line. This act, simple and quick, embodies the essence of being proactive - taking a small step now to avoid a larger problem later.

Let's delve into an analogy to clarify this concept further. Imagine your bathroom is a garden. Gardens thrive with regular attention - a bit of weeding here, some pruning there. Neglect it for too long, and you'll find yourself with an overgrown, unruly mess that takes much more effort to tidy up. Similarly, by adopting an approach that takes care of messes as they occur, you're essentially 'weeding' your bathroom regularly, ensuring it remains a pleasant and manageable space.

Such habits don't require extensive effort; many are simple incorporations into your daily routine that make a significant impact over time. It starts with adopting the mindset that every small action contributes to a larger goal of maintaining a clean and inviting bathroom space.

The key to maintaining a clean bathroom with minimal effort is developing proactive cleaning habits that address messes promptly.

Mastering Effortless Bathroom Maintenance

Bathroom maintenance shouldn't feel like an uphill battle. The secret lies in smart strategies that weave cleaning tasks into the rhythm of your daily life, making them almost unnoticeable yet incredibly effective.

Consider the power of a cleaning schedule. Rather than dedicating a single day to cleaning your bathroom from top to bottom—a daunting task that's easy to postpone—break it down into smaller, manageable tasks spread across the week. For example, Monday might be for decluttering countertops, while Wednesday is reserved for scrubbing the shower. This approach reduces the workload on any given day and ensures every part of your bathroom receives regular attention, reducing the chance of dirt and grime build-up.

Implementing the right tools within arm's reach is another game-changer. Having cleaning supplies readily available encourages you to tackle a spot before it becomes a stubborn stain. This convenience eliminates the barrier of having to fetch supplies from another room, which often is the moment the decision to "do it later" creeps in.

Incorporating these strategies into your routine can be as seamless as integrating a new habit into your life. At first, it might require a conscious effort, but soon, it becomes second nature. Like embedding a new app on your smartphone that swiftly becomes essential, these bathroom maintenance strategies will blend into your daily life, becoming indispensable for preserving cleanliness and hygiene.

Imagine your bathroom as a serene sanctuary that remains perpetually clean, not through laborious effort but through the effortless integration of smart habits into your lifestyle. This vision is not only achievable but sustainable with the right approach to bathroom maintenance.

Could the path to a perpetually pristine bathroom be as simple as weaving maintenance tasks into the fabric of your daily routine?

Implementing Organizational Systems

An organized bathroom is both visually appealing and functionally superior. To achieve and maintain this state requires the implementation of organizational systems that support ongoing cleanliness. This strategy transcends mere tidiness; it is about creating an environment where everything has its place, and cleanliness becomes an inherent component of the room.

Start with decluttering. Removing excess items and keeping only what's necessary can drastically improve the bathroom's functionality and appearance. This initial step makes it easier to designate specific spots for all your bathroom essentials, from toiletries to cleaning supplies. The fewer items you have to manage, the simpler it is to keep everything in order.

Consider incorporating clever storage solutions to maximize space and maintain order. Drawer organizers, over-the-door hooks, and under-sink storage bins are just a few examples that can transform chaos into harmony. By giving every item a designated home, you reduce clutter on countertops and in shower spaces, making regular cleaning tasks quicker and more efficient.

Here's an analogy to bring this concept to life: Think of your bathroom as a library. Just as books are categorized and shelved to be easily found, your bathroom essentials should be systematically organized to ensure smooth, daily operations. This not only makes cleaning faster but also makes using and enjoying your bathroom a more pleasant experience.

Adopting these organizational systems does not have to be an overhaul performed in one day. Gradual implementation and tweaking to fit your needs and habits will yield a personalized system that works effortlessly for you, transforming bathroom maintenance from a chore into a simple part of your routine.

Embracing proactive cleaning habits, integrating maintenance tasks into your daily life, and implementing organizational systems are the three pillars to maintaining a consistently clean bathroom with minimal effort.

Embrace a Proactive Mindset

Don't wait for messes to pile up. Address them as they happen. Remember, a small stain today can turn into a stubborn mark tomorrow. *Procrastination leads to accumulation.* By taking a few minutes each day to tackle spills, soap scum, or stray hairs, you prevent them from becoming major cleaning undertakings later.

Stay Ahead of the Game

Consistency is key to cleanliness. Make it a habit to incorporate cleaning tasks into your daily routine. Whether it's wiping down surfaces after use or quickly tidying up clutter, these small efforts go a long way in maintaining a sparkling bathroom. *Commit to a schedule that fits your lifestyle.* It might seem like a little extra work now, but the payoff is a bathroom that always looks its best.

Organize for Efficiency

A place for everything, and everything in its place. Establish organizational systems that support your cleaning efforts. Invest in storage solutions like baskets or shelves to keep items off countertops. *Maximize space by decluttering regularly.* When everything has its designated spot, cleaning becomes easier and more streamlined.

10

The Bigger Picture: A Refuge of Freshness

She stood there, a figure framed by the doorway, her gaze sweeping over the gleaming porcelain and the clean lines of her bathroom. Each tile, a testament to the countless scrubbing, shone under the soft glow of the afternoon sun that filtered through the window. She could feel the clean air permeate, and it seemed to settle upon her chest, lighter than before.

The woman had known spaces crowded with neglect, where mildew's musk replaced the crispness of cleanliness. Those had been times of closed doors and excuses made too quickly. But here, in this sanctuary, she found a purer sort of solitude that resonated with the steady beating of her heart.

Reflections danced across the mirror, not marred by water spots or the toothpaste splatters of rushed mornings. She allowed herself a small smile, one that touched her eyes and eased the tightness in her shoulders. This was a canvas of her making, a silent symphony of order and calm.

Her hands, with their slightly reddened knuckles evidence of her labor, brushed against the soft, neatly folded towels. They whispered a promise of comfort and care, as she had whispered promises to herself in the days when the depression had hung heavy on her frame. She felt the echo of that time, a shadow passing as quickly as it came.

Just yesterday, a friend had commented on the airiness of her abode, the welcoming warmth that seemed to embrace visitors upon entry. They had not seen the disarray that used to preside; they did not know of the evenings spent cocooned in her own desolation, afraid to move and disturb the dust that marked her stillness.

A clean bathroom, a simple triumph over the gloom that threatened to settle within her. It was more than aesthetics; it was a victory, a loud proclamation that here was health, wellness, a testament to the resilience of the human spirit.

And, as she replaced the hand soap with a deliberate gentleness, as if setting a jewel into its rightful place, one couldn't help but wonder: Does the space we inhabit reflect the health of the soul, and can the meticulous care of our surroundings help heal the wounds we carry?

A Refuge of Freshness Awaits

Imagine stepping into your bathroom, a place often associated with the mundane task of cleansing, and instead finding a haven that rejuvenates not just the body, but the mind and spirit as well. This is not a distant reality or a luxury reserved for spa retreats, but a tangible, achievable state for your very own home. The journey through "Sparkle and Shine," culminates in understanding that a clean bathroom does more than just sparkle—it impacts your health, happiness, and overall life satisfaction in profound ways.

The importance of cleanliness, especially in a bathroom, extends far beyond aesthetics. It's a **critical component of a healthy home environment**. Bacteria and mold thrive in the moist, warm conditions of a bathroom, posing potential health risks that can be mitigated through regular cleaning practices. But the benefits of a clean bathroom don't stop at health. They ripple out, affecting our mental well-being and our perceptions of our living spaces. When your bathroom sparkles, it's not just the surfaces that shine; **your home**

becomes a more inviting, peaceful place for you and your guests.

Maintaining cleanliness in your bathroom can seem daunting, especially for beginners. However, learning essential bathroom cleaning techniques and incorporating them into a weekly routine makes this monumental task not only manageable but also surprisingly satisfying. The sense of accomplishment from transforming a space from grimy to gleaming cannot be understated. It's about more than just cleanliness; it's about **creating an environment that supports and enhances your well-being**.

A sparkling bathroom serves as a visual metaphor for control and order in one's life, contributing significantly to overall **life satisfaction**. It's a small, personal space where one starts and ends the day, making its condition inherently linked to daily mood and outlook. A clean, well-maintained bathroom can provide a sense of freshness and renewal each morning, setting a positive tone for the day ahead.

The connection between bathroom aesthetics and wellness is unmistakable. From the calming effect of uncluttered countertops to the invigorating sensation of stepping onto a spotless floor, every detail contributes to a nurturing environment. This creates a sanctuary, not just for physical cleansing, but for mental and emotional rejuvenation as well.

Creating this sanctuary doesn't require endless hours or expensive products. It's about adopting simple, efficient routines that ensure your bathroom remains a space that brings joy, health, and satisfaction into your life. With the insights and techniques shared throughout this book, the seemingly ordinary task of cleaning transforms into an act of care for your home and yourself.

The journey towards a glistening bathroom teaches a broader lesson about the impact of our surroundings on our well-being. It's a reminder that investing time in our spaces is not just about maintaining property value or appearances; **it's about nurturing places that sustain and refresh us.** As you embrace the practices discussed, remember, the goal is not just to clean—it's to create a refuge of freshness that elevates the quality of your life.

Comprehend the Deeper Impact of a Clean Bathroom on Health and Wellness

A clean bathroom goes beyond the sparkle and gleam that meets the eye. It is a sanctuary where health and wellness start. Each wipe and scrub removes potential harmful microbes and dust that can affect our respiratory health. The absence of these unwanted guests in our bathroom significantly reduces the risk of allergies and infections, making our homes safer for everyone, especially for those with compromised immune systems.

Imagine your bathroom as a garden. Just as weeds and pests can hinder the growth of healthy plants, dirt and bacteria in a bathroom can impede our health and wellness. Regular cleaning is akin to gardening - removing the unwanted, nurturing the desirable, and fostering a space that encourages health and growth.

Studies have shown that the presence of mold and mildew, which thrive in damp environments like bathrooms, can lead to respiratory issues and worsen conditions such as asthma. Regular cleaning can prevent the buildup of these harmful organisms, keeping the air in your bathroom fresh and clean. This effort not only promotes physical health but also impacts our mental wellbeing by creating a space that feels cared for and under control.

Exploring further, there's a psychological aspect to a clean bathroom as well. A tidy and hygienic bathroom environment can minimize stress and promote feelings of tranquility. After a long day, a clean bathroom offers a sense of refreshment and calm. The organization and cleanliness of the environment can reflect internally, promoting a clearer, more peaceful mind.

The true essence of a clean bathroom lies not just in its visual appeal, but in its role as a foundation for

the health and wellness of those who use it.

Learn How Maintaining Bathroom Cleanliness Can Contribute to a Happier and More Inviting Home

An inviting home is characterized by spaces that are not only visually appealing but also emotionally welcoming. The bathroom, often overlooked, plays a critical role in this equation. Regular cleaning and maintenance transform it from merely a functional space to one that contributes greatly to the overall happiness of a home.

Consider the bathroom as the heart of the home's hygiene. Just as a heart pumps blood to keep the body alive, a clean bathroom pumps vitality into the home, fostering a happier and healthier environment for inhabitants and visitors alike. It's a private retreat, a space where the day's stresses can be washed away, and tranquility can be found. This nurturing environment becomes a source of daily renewal and refreshment.

In fact, a study found that individuals who described their living spaces as "cluttered" or full of "unfinished projects" were more likely to feel depressed and fatigued. In contrast, those who kept their homes clean were more likely to report feeling joyful and energetic. The psychology behind cleanliness taps into our deep need for order and harmony. A well-maintained bathroom speaks of care and attention, qualities that deeply impact our emotional well-being.

Imagine the feeling of walking into a bathroom that's clean, organized, and refreshingly scented. This experience can significantly boost your mood, providing a subtle yet profound sense of well-being. The care put into maintaining such a space radiates warmth and hospitality, making everyone feel welcome and cared for.

A clean bathroom also sets a standard of excellence within the home, encouraging other positive habits and routines. It serves as a model for cleanliness and organization, inspiring similar attention and care to other areas of the house. This ripple effect can elevate the overall atmosphere of a home, making it a more delightful place to live.

How might transforming your bathroom into a haven of cleanliness and order influence the happiness and well-being of your entire household?

Understand the Connection Between Bathroom Aesthetics and Overall Life Satisfaction

The aesthetics of a bathroom — its design, cleanliness, and ambiance — play a significant role in our overall life satisfaction. Much like a piece of art, a well-kept bathroom can evoke feelings of pleasure and contentment. Its cleanliness and order contribute not only to physical health but also to mental and emotional wellness.

Evidence suggests that environments that are clean and aesthetically pleasing can lead to higher levels of happiness and reduced stress. In the context of a bathroom, this means that its appearance and state of cleanliness can significantly affect how we start and end our days. A serene and pleasing bathroom environment can set a positive tone for the day ahead and provide a comforting retreat at day's end.

Consider the bathroom as a mirror reflecting the care we take in our personal and environmental well-being. A dirty and cluttered bathroom can mirror and reinforce feelings of disorder and neglect, whereas a clean and aesthetically pleasing bathroom reflects order, self-care, and pride in one's living space.

Moreover, investing time in the cleanliness and design of a bathroom can serve as a form of self-expression and creativity. It allows individuals to create a space that reflects their personal style and needs, further enhancing their connection to their home and, by extension, their satisfaction with their living situation.

Understanding the deeper value of a clean bathroom helps us see that it's not just about aesthetics; it's about creating a space that uplifts our health,

happiness, and overall life satisfaction. A sparkling bathroom fosters a hygienic environment, conveys care and attention, and contributes to a happier, more inviting home. Ultimately, the state of our bathrooms can reflect and influence the state of our lives.

Reflection

As we close this chapter on the deeper significance of a clean bathroom, it's crucial to reflect on the profound impact it has on our lives. **A clean bathroom is not just about appearances; it's about creating a sanctuary within our homes where freshness and wellbeing intertwine.** By understanding how the cleanliness of our bathroom can influence our health, happiness, and overall satisfaction with life, we can truly appreciate the value of this often-overlooked space.

Moving Forward

Maintaining a sparkling bathroom is a commitment to yourself and your loved ones. It's a small yet meaningful act that can have far-reaching effects on your daily life. As you continue on your journey to a glistening bathroom, remember that each scrub and polish is an investment in your well-being and the harmony of your home.

Final Thoughts

In the grand tapestry of life, the bathroom may seem like a minor thread, but its role should not be underestimated. **A well-kept bathroom is not just a reflection of cleanliness; it is a mirror of your dedication to self-care and your environment.** As you revel in the newfound freshness of your bathroom, take pride in the transformation you've initiated. Let this be a springboard to other aspects of your life, where small steps can lead to significant changes.

From Sparkle to Shine: A Journey to Confidence

As we wrap up our time together, think of this journey not just in terms of transforming your bathroom but as a **bold first step towards a more confident you**. This book was crafted with love and care, addressing not just the surface level of cleaning, but aiming to reach deeper, touching the heart of why we care for our spaces and ourselves.

Bringing the Lessons Home

The real magic of what we've discussed isn't confined to the pages of a book. It's in the **practical application** of each technique, tip, and trick into your daily life. Imagine the sense of accomplishment after quickly tackling a mess you once thought daunting, or the pride in having a home ready to welcome guests at a moment's notice. The methods shared here are more than just cleaning techniques; they are your toolkit for cultivating an environment that bolsters confidence, promotes well-being, and supports your lifestyle.

Recap with a Sparkle

Let's quickly reflect on the **key takeaways** from our time together:

- **Simplicity is power.** Effective cleaning doesn't require an arsenal of products or hours of your time.

- **Routine is your friend.** Small, consistent efforts can prevent overwhelming tasks.

- **Mindfulness in cleaning** transforms a chore into an act of care for your home and yourself.

Remember, the goal was never just about achieving a gleaming bathroom; it's about creating a space that reflects **the best version of yourself.**

Taking Action

Now, with these insights, I encourage you to **create a personalized cleaning schedule** that doesn't overwhelm but empowers you. Adapt the techniques that resonated most and integrate them into your day or week. Don't hesitate to experiment—discovery is part of the process.

Embrace Limitations, Anticipate Growth

Yes, this guide focuses on the bathroom, perhaps a narrow scope, but it's a crucial starting point. There's always more to explore, from deep cleaning strategies to organizing masterclasses. Treat each limitation as an invitation for further learning and exploration.

A Call to Shine

I urge you to **take this knowledge, shine up your space, and in doing so, polish your confidence**. Let each spray, scrub, and sweep remind you that you are capable of creating positive change, starting with the corners of your own world.

As we conclude, carry with you the understanding that the condition of your space does not define you but caring for it can reflect and affect your inner state in powerful ways. Consider this journey a step toward not just a cleaner home, but a brighter, more vibrant life.

"The objective of cleaning is not just to clean, but to feel happiness living within that environment." - Marie Kondo

Let that happiness be your guide, from the corners of your bathroom to the expanse of your life. Shine on.